JAEL THE CONQUEROR

BISHOP DONALD R DOWNING

Jael The Conqueror

© 2023 by Donald R. Downing

Published in Hampton, VA, by Fruition Publishing Concierge Services®. Fruition Publishing Concierge Services® is a division of Alesha Brown, LLC.

Fruition Publishing Concierge Services® can bring authors to your live event. For more information or to book an event, visit Fruition Publishing Concierge Services® at

www.FruitionPublishing.com

First edition published 2009. Second edition 2023.

ISBN: 978-1-954486-47-8 Paperback

ISBN: 978-1-954486-48-5 eBook

Library of Congress Control Number: 2023913203

Unless otherwise noted, all scriptures are from The Holy Bible, King James Version. (1979). Cambridge Edition.

DEDICATION

This book is dedicated to my Lord and Savior Jesus Christ, who brought me out of the fiery furnace, saw me through my lowest valleys, cloudy days, and difficult times: who has revealed Jael in my spirit and has given me the grace to write this story about her life.

To my wife and best friend, Evangelist Lezlie Downing, you are the Jael of my life. I thank you for 22 years of faith and encouragement.

To my Heart to Heart Church Family Worldwide, remember that a day hemmed in prayer will never unravel.

To my daughter, Stephanie, as you go forth in life, keep faith in the .com of your life and God's Word within the hard drive of your heart.

To every woman who has been persecuted in ministry, held back in society by men, and treated as lesser, weaker vessels in Christ, this one is for you!

TABLE OF CONTENTS

THE PURPOSE OF THIS BOOK

This book is to bring to light and celebrate the remarkable story of Jael: a woman of God, blessed above, and a Kenite maiden who delivered Israel from wicked bondage. She has not been given her rightful place in church history or in modern-day theological teachings of biblical heroes such as David, Moses, Deborah, Ruth, and Joshua. I attribute this error to the fact that Jael was not a Jewish maiden but was of Kenite ancestry.

Christian societies in every nation have not brought the story of Jael to the forefront of the Gospel as other biblical characters, even though she was mightily used by God. Some reasons are because the cold fingers of racism are still prevalent in the heart of the End Times Church.

It is never the color of one's skin that determines eternal life but the condition of one's heart. Man looks at the outward appearance, but God looks at the heart. The Lord said this to Samuel: "Do not look on his countenance or on the height of his stature because I have refused him; for the Lord seeth not as man seeth; for man looketh on the outward appearance, but the Lord looketh on the heart (1 Samuel 16:7, NKJV)."

While Judges Chapters 4 and 5 tell the story of a black Kenite woman, I have built and expanded the story through research, vision, and inspiration from the Holy Spirit. God's heroine Jael is a pre-David and Goliath narrative that will encourage you to ascend to the highest level of becoming the most blessed. This book will prove that God wants to bless His people richly, and that He is still no respecter of persons, but will bless and keep every heart that has been perfected for His purpose, regardless of gender or ethnic background.

Jael, the Kenite maiden blessed above, came home to the true and living God, even though we can be sure she was scorned, rebuked, persecuted, and cast down by others of her race. This book invites all non-Jewish people in the world today to be as Jael and come home to the Father of Life in Jesus Christ. Home is where the Father is. If you are Jewish, I invite you to consider the fact that the Father is in Christ (John 14:7-11) and that we all must be Father-filled, Son-washed, and Holy Spirit-preserved.

As David stood before the giant Goliath, Jael stood before the wicked giant Sisera. In both cases, the salvation of Israel was on the line. David had an army of men behind him as he stood before Goliath, but Jael had no one except her faith and God's favor.

Now is the time for the modern-day Jaels on the earth to rise up and kill the devil and to walk in their rightly blessed above position, putting on the whole armor of God and tearing down those spiritual Jericho walls. Many unlearned male leaders, in error, have tried to build walls around the women of God, especially those who labor night and day in a Full Gospel ministry. This bondage and mentality have sown much disunity in the body of Christ.

Yes, it is a breakthrough time for today's Jaels: time to rise up and slay today's Siseras of bondage, doubt, unbelief, intimidation, and fear. It is time to walk in total victory, being blessed by God above and excelling to the elite level of the most blessed of all.

Come forth now, Jael, O mighty woman of God, and encompass all of your blessings. Be blessed above and prosper in the midst of your trials, troubles, temptations, persecutions, and storms. Enter God's presence with a pure and clean heart, wearing the whole armor of God. Establish right thoughts and imaginations with a pure and sound mind of Christ. If you are on the brink of a mighty blessing, allow this book to push you over.

INTRODUCTION

In the last days, God has been doing great things on the earth, but mankind is still not aware of it. Through much teaching, preaching, and holding strictly to many doctrines and beliefs of men, we know what God has said but have failed to hear what He is now saying. We have ceased to be able to discern the inward voice of God from the voice of our own spirit. In addition, we desperately need the Holy Spirit to direct the teachers in what they should be teaching us.

We have been a religious society that wants to know God only in the realm of His blessings and not as servants, laborers, warriors, and witnesses for the Gospel of Jesus Christ. In ignorance, we judge people by the color of their skin, gender, wealth, or countenance and not by the condition of their hearts. This is not good.

All of us are guilty. We want God to do what we ask, yet we refuse to do what He asks. We are still divided by our traditions and comfort zones and locked in the pride of being in denominations that fail to see the inward wars and battles of our very own hearts. We are continually building great buildings, but God is building great hearts. We count bodies, but the Lord counts hearts.

We also fail to see the persecution of women servants of God have endured and are going through worldwide. They, too, are being mightily used by God in the ministration so that many people are richly blessed. God used a woman to give birth to every man, even His only begotten Son, the Lord Jesus Christ. Most men still fail to see that the biblical terms He, Him, and His include the female species as well.

In Genesis 5:2, God called them Adam. The Apostle Paul in Romans 8:14 gives strength to the oneness of male and female, saying: "For as many as are led by the Spirit of God, they are Sons of God." Therefore, spiritually speaking, a woman is a Son of God, just as a man is the Bride of Christ. Our God is an Equal Opportunity Savior. All He requires is repentance and a pure and clean heart.

Few Biblical studies and teachings have come forth in Christianity about the mighty Kenite nation where Jael was born. Yet, they lived in Canaan during the time of Abraham (Genesis 15:19). They were metal craftsmen and were there at the time of Israel's Exodus from Egypt and showed them much kindness (1 Samuel 15:6).

In fact, Moses' father-in-law, Jethro, was called a Kenite (Judges 1:16). Many scholars believe that the skill in smelting and casting the golden calf (Exodus 32) and the bronze serpent (Numbers 21) came from the presence of the Kenites. In the kingdom of hearts, there is no lesser or greater race, but one body called Christ.

The Kenites were among the Israelites who entered the Promised Land in the conquest led by Joshua (Judges 1:16). Yet their nation has been excluded from much of church history. In 1 Samuel 15:8, King Saul was sent by God to destroy the Amalekites and Amalek, their king. He told the Kenites to depart from among the Amalekites, and they obeyed. Heber, Jael's husband, was also a Kenite who had favor with Jabin, the king. The nation would produce one of the greatest ethnic women of the Bible, whom God used as Israel's deliverer. I call her Jael the Conqueror.

It surprised me greatly when several theologians spoke of Jael as if she was a murderer. Some of the current Bible dictionaries alluded that after she killed Sisera, Jael called out to Barak and showed him where Sisera lay dead in her tent so that she would be glorified among women. Some dared to imply that the prophetic word spoken by Deborah—that Sisera would die at the hands of a woman—was just a coincidence when it came to pass. In ignorance, these so-called theologians believed God did not divinely inspire Jael's actions.

I disagree with these teachings because the Kenite tribe mixing with the 12 tribes of Israel is how Jael became God's great servant, chosen and saved. In Hebrew, the name Jael means a mountain goat or one that is very swift and dwells above in high places. Jael being "Blessed above Women" perfectly fits her being chosen and used by God for His divine purpose.

Any hunter will tell you that it's very difficult to catch a wild mountain goat, for it dwells upon impossibly high cliffs and is very cunning, quick, and extremely intelligent. I believe that Jael, too, dwelled in the high places of "The Rock" and that Rock was Christ. Many women today dwell in that same place. "And did all drink the spiritual drink; for they drank of that spiritual Rock that followed them: and that Rock was Christ" (1 Corinthians 10:4).

Despite her ancestry, Jael served, believed, and lived unto the God of the Jews. God used her to deliver His people from the evil Sisera, just as He used David to deliver His people from the giant Goliath.

This book, inspired by the Holy Spirit of God, tells about the exploits of Jael, "Blessed above Women." In her time, Jael delivered the women of Canaan from religious bondage, male persecution, and laws against women set up by men, who believed that a woman's life was just to please the man, serve the man, and raise the children.

After the death of Sisera, Jael became well known and respected by both sexes. In my heart, I believe that she and her husband, Heber, brought forth equal rights for all women of Canaan.

This book is meant to encourage all to put their time in for God and punch in on God's time clock for a great eternal paycheck. We must not allow our past to dictate our future. We must monitor how we spend our time and become focused on our lifetime. We must know what God is downloading on the hard drive of our hearts and printing in the infrastructure of our minds.

Let us pray:

> *Heavenly Father, we thank You for our most blessed position and for our being highly favored in Your presence. Thank You for Your many bless-ings and the reward that is in Your hands that You hold in reserve for all who love You. Thank You for revealing the story of Jael blessed above women, thus letting us know that You are no respecter of persons, but the One True God of both Jew and Gentile, the One True God, Lord of all, and King of Kings. Bless those, dear Lord, who will read this book, that they may understand all that is of You, what it is You would have all of us do upon this earth, and how to receive our eternal great reward. We thank You in the precious matchless name of our Lord and Savior, Jesus Christ. Amen.*

CHAPTER I

COMMENTS FROM THE AUTHOR:

J ael was God's servant, just like Moses, Abraham, and David. Jabin and Sisera were servants of sin, self, and Satan. David, by his relationship and faith in God, not only had the courage to run forward to slay Goliath with a slingshot and a stone, but I believe he had the same spirit as Jael the Kenite maiden, who stood before the evil Sisera as fearless, trusting in God.

Even though they were giants, Sisera and Goliath's humanistic mistake was the same that many make today. We see our strength as finite muscle and bone, not infinite wisdom, knowledge, and heart, through a firm relationship with God.

Even though Jael did slay him, in the eyes of God, he was already spiritually dead due to his sinful lifestyle, which is the worst death of all. He walked as a giant among men but was less than a child, being used in the hands of the devil. As he worked for Jabin, the king, he didn't see the demonic spirit working in him and through him, leading to an early grave and eternal judgment.

Jael's power was her faith in God and His promises. Sisera had some strength in his title as captain, yet his weakness of greed, fleshly desires, and wicked heart were greater. Readers beware! David wrote about this story in the book of Psalm (83:9-10): "Do unto them as unto the Midianites; as to Sisera, as to Jabin, at the brook of Kishon: which perished at Endor they became as dung for the earth."

Let's look at the heart of Sisera, Jabin the king, Jael, Deborah, and Barak. Each heart was the key element that produced the story of Jael from the beginning to the end. Their hearts determined their endings. The condition of our hearts ultimately determines the wages of sin.

All must obey God's Word and possess a pure and clean heart. Why is this? We can never be any more than what our heart is.

Our hearts determine eternal life, faith, love, and the power of God's Word in our daily life. It is His address and residence on the Earth, His dwelling place (2 Corinthians 6:16-18). If there is no obedience, repentance, and faith from the heart, the price of sin will be required as our eternal life payment in the end. In other words, the more we sin upon the Earth, the less we shall receive in glory. We must work and obey from the heart.

"But God be thanked, that you were the servants of sin, but you have obeyed from the heart that form of doctrine which was delivered to you (Romans 6:17, KJ2000)."

By our labors of witnessing to the lost, helping the poor and the needy, and working in the local assembly and in the family, we gather valuable fruit unto eternal life: a sure reward, a great harvest.

Our Lord works with us and through us for His eternal purpose. There are wages of righteousness and wages of unrighteousness. All that we sow, we shall surely reap.

Men require high titles, ordination, and a license if one is to move into a higher religious position, but God requires love, relationship, and a pure and clean heart. In error, many magnify their million-dollar titles, such as Apostle, Prophet, Evangelist, and Teacher, while possessing a five-dollar heart within themselves.

Religious mankind has taken great titles just to rule over others, to build their own kingdoms and religions, causing spiritual heart attacks and Gospel strokes to occur in the body of Christ. No religious degree or title is ever greater than bowed knees and clean hearts! It is not always what we see in Christ that is most important, but what God sees within us.

It is time to take up our cross (Luke 9:23; 14:27), put on the whole armor of God (Ephesians 6:10-18), use our spiritual weapons, and kill the devil and his giant Siseras of covetousness, lust, false religion, and disobedience. Our missionaries often must be transformed into warring mercenaries, and every believer a spiritual killing machine. No, we do not seek to kill anyone physically, but those evil spirits that war against God's purpose, causing sin and sickness in the body of Christ, must be destroyed.

Ignorance can never take us where our faith wants us to go. In the Old Testament, war was very physical, but in the New Testament, it is very spiritual, especially those personal secret wars of the heart. Today, God is looking for spiritual Jaels who are not afraid of the giant Siseras in the church or in the world.

We are the servants of Christ in action and servants who are joint heirs with Christ in an eternal position. Christ took on the form of a servant. Philippians 2:7: "But made Himself of no reputation, and took upon him the form of a servant, and was made in the likeness of men."

Just as Christ was made in our likeness and image, we must be made (transformed) into His likeness and image for God's kingdom on Earth, transformed from adults to children of God (Matthew 18:2-3; Romans 12:2) and from humanity to godliness.

By her labor, love, and heart for God, Jael earned wages and a reward of eternal life. By his works, Sisera earned eternal condemnation and judgment.

Eternal condemnation and judgment are eternal death, total separation from God. The unsaved are considered dead while they yet live on Earth. All accountable-age persons have a history of work they have done, and that work has a payment due, which carries eternal benefits.

Now I must point out the critical point to be learned from Jael in this book. It is all about the condition of the heart, what is there, and who dwells there within us.

We must put off our *old man Sisera*, and put on the Lord Jesus Christ, that we may be saved. "But put ye on the Lord Jesus Christ, and make not provision for the flesh, to fulfill the lusts thereof (Romans 13:14)." (See also Galatians 3:27-28).

I believe the greatest title available is one that is least sought after by man: the title of a servant. Jael, Barak, and Deborah were God's servants. There is simply no greater title that will produce a greater eternal reward for us than that of a servant.

Before Jesus Christ could be found pleasing and approved by God, He had to first become a faithful and willing servant. Being servants of God, we do not live in sin. We work diligently and daily unto God to obtain a great eternal reward. Sinning servants will destroy all their good works of faith and eternal reward.

We must "awake to righteousness and sin not (1 Corinthians 15:34a)." We must not allow our sinful past to dictate our heavenly future, "for the wages of sin is death…(Romans 6:23a)."

What we need to assure us of our expected end is a washed heart. "O Jerusalem, wash thine heart from wickedness, that thou may be saved (Jeremiah 4:14a)." We wash our hearts by God's Word (John 15:3) and by faith (Acts 15:9). And by the blood of the Lord Jesus Christ, the Lamb of God (Revelation 1:5-6).

We all must be washed and cleaned up to go up. All the facts are in, and none, regardless of religious beliefs, can deny the evidence that there is an empty tomb in Jerusalem. This is because Jesus Christ has risen and is now seated as Lord of Lords and King of Kings.

CHAPTER 2

IN CANAAN LAND, A FEMALE WARRIOR IS BORN

Zamu and Hadassah were very excited. Hadassah was pregnant and expected to give birth to their first child at any moment. Zamu wanted a son, but Hadassah wanted a girl.

When Hadassah went into labor, her sister Modessa ran for the midwife. Less than three hours later, a baby girl was born. Zamu was disappointed at first, and then he was happy upon seeing the lovely child lying in Modessa's arms.

"What shall we name her?" He asked.

After much debating between themselves, they named her Jael in honor of her Aunt Modessa, who was almost four cubits tall, a woman who possessed uncommon strength, virtue, honor, and ability that surpassed most men.

Modessa belonged to a group of people who did not live like the other Canaanites. Some of them were warriors, male and female. Others were scholars who believed that everyone should be able to read, write, and cipher, whether male or female, rich or poor—not just the priests and scribes.

Modessa's friends even included some Levites and scribes who had left the Israelites in search of knowledge about their Canaanite neighbors. Modessa was trained in secret practices of self-defense and hand-to-hand combat that only temple warriors and high-ranking mercenaries knew.

Although Zamu felt that Modessa was a little strange, he knew Hadassah loved her. Modessa's friends had helped him several times, sharing healing knowledge that the priests ordinarily kept to themselves, explaining to him the cycles of planting and harvesting to get a better yield from his crops. He held Modessa in the highest regard and felt he owed her his life.

Once, he was out in the countryside, far from the closeted walled cities, when a lion chased him. Zamu ran for his life, and when he thought all was lost, Modessa appeared and thrust her spear into the lion's heart. She told him that Jehovah, the God of the Israelites, had sent her to protect him.

Soon after that, Hadassah discovered she was pregnant. Zamu felt it only right to honor Modessa in the naming of her niece—without her saving his life, Jael might not have been conceived.

As the child Jael grew, Zamu taught her as he would a son, and Hadassah taught her all the skills a well-brought-up young woman needed to know. Though Zamu had some misgivings, he did not interfere when Modessa took the girl to her home in the next village for long visits.

Modessa taught Jael to read, write, cipher, and use swords, knives, spears, and bows. Jael listened and asked questions when her scholarly and priestly friends gathered to speak of the many gods of Israel, Egypt, Canaan, Assyria, and Babylon.

Two things amazed Zamu and Hadassah: Jael's physical strength and quickness in all that she did. By the age of six, she could clean the house, wash clothes, and all the dirty dishes as quickly as her mother, Hadassah. Her passion was remarkable, and she exceeded in wisdom above her peers.

Her father boasted to all his friends that Jael was far better than a son. She had a gift for working with the horses that her father raised and trained; she could often calm a frightened or angry horse so that Zamu was able to tame and train it. She never complained or disobeyed her parents and always tried to honor others.

As Jael grew and went to the shrines to worship on holy days or participated in festivals to mark the seasons, she learned the stories that explained the beliefs of her people, the Kenites, and the Canaanites of the surrounding towns. She learned the legends of how Baal built the temple and how King Keret of Hubur lost his family in a tribal war and plague, and the adventures and battles of the many gods and goddesses—Baal, Ashtoreth, El, Asherah, Molech, and others. She heard tales of the gods and goddesses of Egypt and Assyria from the merchants and slave traders who came through the nearby towns.

Jael liked best to hear the stories from her aunt's Levite friend, Joab, about Yahweh, the God of the Hebrews who had slowly infiltrated the land of Canaan in the last few generations. They claimed their God, also called Jehovah, was the only true God who made the entire world and everything within it.

Yahweh wanted His people to live pure lives and demanded justice and righteousness from them. Jael liked what she heard about the Hebrews' God and wanted to learn more. She learned to recognize the clan markings of the Levites, an entire tribe set aside to serve Jehovah. Whenever she saw a Levite and her errands for her parents allowed the time, she would ask the Levite to teach her more about his God.

When she was old enough, Jael refused to participate in the annual feasts to the false gods her parents worshipped. She wanted to worship and serve the Holy God of Israel, even though Jabin the king and Sisera the Giant held Israel in bondage.

BEZER THE BULLY

Everyone in the village loved Jael, except Bezer, a bully who tormented all the village girls and even made adults fearful of him. Often, he would chase the young girls to pull their hair and dirty their clothes. He would push other young boys around and dare anyone to fight him. Bezer was very large for his age and stood a full head taller than everyone else his age in the village.

Not only did Bezer steal food and throw rocks to break water jars and throw clean laundry into the dirt, but he also cut the hobbles of donkeys and frightened grazing cattle and threw dye–stolen from the weaver's house–onto the sheep in the field to ruin their wool before shearing. He played nasty tricks on anyone he couldn't frighten, tossing live spiders and lizards into kneading troughs of women baking their families' bread or dust into the wine cups of men sitting in the tavern.

No one cared for Bezer the Bully. He tried his best to intimidate young Jael, but to his surprise, she showed no fear. He often thought about grabbing her long, beautiful hair and pulling it out by the roots, yet something deep inside seemed to restrain him and instinctively warn him of her inner strength and power.

Several years went by, and there came a day of reckoning for Bezer the Bully. He had grown taller, had gained weight, and extended his bullying from the village to the surrounding countryside.

Bezer was having a bad day. He had been apprenticed to the village blacksmith with plans to become wealthy and powerful and someday come to the king's attention. But on that day, his master had berated him in front of all the important men of the village—important men Bezer could not bully. They had laughed at him.

Then, to make matters worse, the girl he wanted to court told him in front of half the village that she would rather be a temple prostitute than become his wife. Still, more people laughed at him. The tavern keeper would not sell Bezer any wine so that he could drink and forget his shame, because Bezer had not paid for wine in two moons.

Bezer stood on the bridge over the Kishon River, staring at the water and thinking about how he could avenge himself on everyone who had shamed him when Jael came to the bridge. Her father sent her to the village to fetch a length of cloth he had ordered as a present for Hadassah, and Jael was running late. She was surprised to see Bezer standing in the middle of the bridge, throwing rocks at the fish below.

She walked faster and as softly as possible, praying to the God of Israel that she could pass Bezer before he realized she was there. As she stepped past him, Bezer reached out, grabbed her hair, and pulled with all of his might. His anger and frustration overcame his common sense and sense of restraint that kept him from tormenting her before.

Jael felt a searing pain like she had never experienced before. Pulled off balance, she fell backward into Bezer's arms, and he grabbed her by the neck to choke her, as he had done to so many other girls. With the speed of a young mountain goat, she stomped his foot as hard as she could. The hard sole of her sandal smashed his bare toes.

Bezer howled and let go of Jael's neck and hair. Faster than the eye could see, Jael leaped upon his back with the speed of a young lion and wrapped his head in a headlock her Aunt Modessa had taught her. Any boy smaller than Bezer would have had his neck broken, but Bezer's size and strength protected him from Jael's fear and rage that day.

Bezer screamed for help as loud as he could before Jael's arm around his neck cut off his air. Choking, he pleaded for mercy. He could not breathe, and Bezer knew he was just a moment from death.

Slowly, Jael's compassion connected with her virtue, and her dignity spoke to her character and honor. She let him breathe but made him promise never to torment anyone smaller than him ever again, obey his master, and honor his parents.

Then Jael made him promise never to tell anyone what had happened upon the bridge because Aunt Modessa had made her promise never to show those secret fighting moves to anyone. If Bezer ever told anyone what she had done to him, he would have to deal with her again.

Gasping for breath, terrified and positive that one of the gods had taken over Jael's body to punish him, Bezer promised to do all that she demanded. To the amazement of everyone in the village, Bezer reformed and soon became the pride of his parents and a much-desired suitor of all the girls of marriage age in the village.

Jael kept the secret of what happened on the bridge and thanked the God of Israel in her prayers. She thought her problems were over once Bezer the Bully had reformed, but they were only beginning.

Soon after she turned sixteen, as she came home from visiting her Aunt Modessa, she heard loud shouting voices and screams from her house. With fear and trembling, Jael quickly ran and hid behind a tree next to her house to see what was happening.

Though she wanted to leap into battle, she knew that was foolish: she had weapons and didn't know how many enemies had attacked her home. In the back of her mind, she heard the tales of her Aunt Modessa and her many warrior friends of fools who wanted to be heroes and leaped into battle without knowledge or weapons and were outnumbered and killed.

A large roving band of Kenite renegades had attacked her home. Jael huddled down in the shadows and watched the men, trying to count them, with a vague idea of racing back to Modessa's home and bringing her warrior friends back with her for a rescue.

She didn't want to leave her parents, though. Then the sounds of screams and destruction grew louder and came from all around, and Jael realized with horror that the renegades were attacking the entire village.

A man settled through the knots of ragged, filthy renegades and went into Zamu and Hadassah's home. Jael nearly gasped aloud when she saw the three scars across his leathery cheek. Tales of the man with those three ugly white scars were told to frighten children into obeying their parents. The leader of this band was the notorious Zabed the Terrible.

Jael heard her mother scream as two men dragged her from the house. Zamu broke past two more men blocking the door to race after his wife. Zabed burst out after him, swinging a scimitar too large for an ordinary man to lift.

Just as Zamu reached to pull Hadassah from her attackers' grasps, Zabed swung hard and fast, chopping off Zamu's head. Hadassah screamed and screamed until Zabed backhanded her, smearing Zamu's splattered blood across her face. She fell backward, and the two men holding her tore at her clothes.

Jael felt rooted to the ground, like part of the tree that hid her from the sight of the men plundering her home. Despite her years of training and her confidence as a warrior, she couldn't move as she watched the two men strip her mother and hold her down as the rest of the men of Zabed's band took turns raping her.

Hadassah fell silent, and Jael covered her face with her hands, weeping silently. The sounds of the men laughing and shouting were drowned out by the thundering of her heart.

Jael felt sick, distraught, and helpless, for she knew she couldn't fight them all. There were just too many of them, and she was afraid they would kill her. Aunt Modessa had taught her long ago when there was no hope of victory, a wise warrior did not risk death but endured to live to see another day and take her revenge.

The sound of the men shouting and laughing softened, and Jael peered around the tree again, afraid they had discovered her hiding place and tried to sneak up on her. She saw that most of the men were leaving, dragging away sacks of the family's possessions, the new ewes, the calves, a jar leaking olive oil in a glistening stream across the settling dust.

From the stables far behind the home, she heard the screams of the horses as Zabed's men herded them away. She swallowed a cry of fury as she realized that her special black colt, named Nightwind, was among the stolen horses.

Zabed strolled over to the bloody, shuddering form of Hadassah. Jael forgot to breathe as Zabed lifted his spear and thrust it straight into Hadassah's heart. Her mother's shriek cut off with a gurgling sound that made Jael's inside churn. She swallowed hard and turned her head away. Jael held her breath until all was silent, and every ruffian had left the ruins of her ravaged home.

She ran into the night to her Aunt Modessa's house as fast as her shaking legs could take her. With tears of grief, pain, and anger, she spilled out the whole story to Modessa. The older woman wept silently and took the girl into her arms to comfort her. After several hours of tears and weeping, both fell into a deep sleep.

CHAPTER 3

ZABED THE TERRIBLE

J ael didn't know how long she had slept, but like a mountain goat, she had a sixth sense of the presence of another. That sense woke her.

Jael leaped straight up out of her bed into a defensive position. She saw before her Modessa, standing in full warrior attire, with a long dagger at her side, a huge shield on her left arm, and a mighty sword in her hand.

It was a new day, just before sunrise.

"Jael," Modessa said in soft tones of grief. "I have been to your home. Everything has burned to the ground from the fires set by Zabed and his men. Your parents are indeed dead. There is nothing left. A young man named Heber asked about you while I was there and wanted to know if you were still alive. He wanted to come here and see you, but I told him to wait, that now was not the time. He said he would see to their funeral rites for you and asked me to tell you that your parents would get the best burial possible. I shall be gone for a few days, Jael. If I do not return in five days…"

Before Modessa could wink an eye, Jael leaped before her, seized Modessa's great dagger, and placed it against her aunt's heart, saying, "I know where you are going, and I'm going with you."

Modessa looked into the eyes of Jael. They were no longer the eyes of a young, innocent girl who should have been thinking of nothing beyond suitors but the eyes of a great warrior. She knew if she moved toward the door, Jael would fight her, even though they greatly loved each other.

"Go get your weapons, Jael. I will wait for you. Yes, you may go with me, and together, somehow, we shall have the victory over Zabed the Terrible. Move quickly!"

Jael dashed into the room where her aunt stored all the weapons of war. She couldn't help but feel relief and compassion, thinking about Heber and his deep concern for her.

She had only seen him several times, and each time there was a strange feeling of tenderness deep within her soul. Quickly, Jael gathered her bow and arrow, a large dagger, and a spear.

Modessa and Jael left just before dawn and went on foot over the mountains, hills, and valleys, traveling much faster than they could have if they had taken horses. There was no need to waste time going back to Jael's home and following the trail left by the ruffians who followed Zabed the Terrible. Modessa had heard the stories and knew their enemies were headed to the mountains of Ziaam.

The Hunt for Zabed the Terrible

Even though Zabed's men had tried to cover their tracks, young Jael could not be fooled. Her aunt had taught her how to follow a trail in the worst conditions, and her skill served her well now when it was so important not to lose the enemy in the foothills and forests.

It was evening when they spied the hoofprints of a large band of horses. Modessa determined they were only a few hours old. Jael said a silent prayer of thanks to the God of Israel. Soon, she would have revenge on her parents' murderers.

Zabed the Terrible knew he was being followed, for he had sent two men of great warring abilities to guard their journey into their secret hiding place. Zabed looked at the men who brought him the news that just two women followed them; a tall, older woman and a slim girl of about fifteen or sixteen.

"Just the age I like them," exclaimed the wicked Zabed.

Confident that two lone women were no threat, Zabed sent all but four of his warriors onward to their secret hiding place in the mountains of Ziaam. He and his remaining warriors turned back and raced to meet what they mistakenly thought would be easy prey.

"Two against five," Zabed said, smiling. "My, my, how good it is to be Zabed the Terrible."

He would let the four men have the older woman, and he would spend the night enjoying himself with the young maiden.

YOUNG JAEL FIGHTS
FOR HER LIFE

"I hear horses coming toward us," Jael exclaimed.

"Come quickly, my child," said Modessa. "Let us set the order of battle. Our enemy must know we are tracking them. I have heard about Zabed the Terrible. He is an arrogant fool. If he knows there are only two of us, he will come against us himself, with only a few warriors."

"It is not just the two of us," Jael said. "I am sure Jehovah God is with us."

"I pray you are right, my dear. I pray that He will strengthen our arms, so no one will ever grieve again because of Zabed the Terrible." Modessa looked around the clear spot on the trail and signaled for Jael to stop.

"They think they will surprise us. Let us surprise them instead." She gestured at the thick clump of trees to one side and dismounted.

Faster than the eye could see, Jael skimmed up a large tree while Modessa vanished between two large boulders.

Meanwhile, Zabed the Terrible did not feel the excitement he thought he should feel with the prospect of rape, terror, and an easy battle ahead of him. It was quiet, and it was getting dark. An eerie chill ran down his evil spine as he thought about death and the hundreds of people he had killed in his lifetime.

From out of nowhere, Modessa's spear and Jael's arrow struck two of his men. They fell from their horses, scrabbling at the weapons that had killed them. As Zabed looked up, Jael came flying out of a nearby tree and down upon him.

From the corner of his eye, Zabed saw Modessa attack his two remaining men like a runaway stallion. Zabed did not have a moment to think, for Jael's spear only missed his throat by a hair's width. The fight was on: Jael, the young warrior, and Zabed the Terrible stood face-to-face.

Zabed attacked with his great sword, and Jael defended herself with a shield and spear. Zabed tried to overpower Jael. He wanted to disable her, not kill her just yet. He wanted to have some fun with her later on.

To his shock, Jael's spear penetrated his defenses and stabbed him deep in the fleshly part of his upper arm. The pain brought Zabed back to reality as Jael followed up her stroke by cutting his left cheek to the bone with the edge of her spear.

Forgetting all else, Zabed fought for his life with all the tricks of his trade. He threw dirt in Jael's face, tried to trip her up, and tried to hit her head with the end of his sword. But as a young lioness preparing to slay her prey, Jael fought with the skill of two men, remembering that this was the man who slaughtered her parents.

Meanwhile, Modessa was busy fighting Zabed's two remaining killers. They were very skilled, evil men who had survived many battles and slain many souls.

As they rushed upon her, Modessa swung rapidly and repeatedly, with weapons in both hands, slashing and gutting her great attackers. She lopped off a hand, then hamstrung off the other man, slashed across the first man's belly, and cut the other's arm to the bone.

Unfortunately, often when a battle seems won, a warrior will misjudge her enemies. Modessa eased up her attack too soon, confident she was already the victor, and it was just a matter of slicing two throats.

The other ruffian went to his knees, pleading for his life. Modessa hesitated for just one moment. Despite her fierceness in battle and the knowledge that this man might have raped her beloved sister before her death, it was not in Modessa to kill in heat and passion.

Suddenly, from within the concealing folds of his ragged shirt, the kneeling man whipped out a large knife and stabbed upward. It went in under her ribs.

Modessa went to her knees, stunned by the pain, gagging on the blood that gushed from her punctured lung. She fought for clarity, drawing her dagger and slashing at the man as he laughed, gloated, and got to his feet too slowly. Eyes wide, he crumpled backward, his life gushing from between his futilely clutching fingers, a gaping wound in his throat.

Only Zabed and Jael were left to fight.

When Jael saw Modessa go down, gurgling blood, she understood the mortality of the wound, and something happened within her. Vengeance overrode her hunger for justice.

Zabed did not deserve a quick death. She played with him, darting in and back out again, delivering cut after painful cut, drawing snarls of pain from her enemy. Soon Zabed's clothes were dark with blood and hung in ribbons from her many cuts. He staggered from blood loss, and his eyes widened in shock. That was enough for her.

She leaped in, slashing with all the finesse of the bull dancers the Cretan priest had described to her one evening long ago. She cut off Zabed's ear.

Zabed lunged after her, staggering as he tried to cut off Jael's left arm with his sword. With the speed of an antelope, she cut off his right hand before driving a dagger through his chest before the cry of pain escaped his throat. Zabed the Terrible was dead before his body hit the ground.

Jael quickly ran to Modessa's side and futilely pushed aside her bloody clothes, hoping to stop the bleeding and save her aunt's life.

"Jael, my dear," Modessa whispered. "You know better. I taught you well. Be proud. We have brought justice for your parents." She smiled as she struggled for breath. Fresh blood dribbled from the corner of her mouth.

"Vengeance for all the innocents Zabed tortured. It's over for me: it's just beginning for you. I go to the God of the Hebrews. Stay with Him, Jael. Serve Him all the days of your life. For He is truly the One True Living God."

Modessa coughed, bringing up a thick, bloody foam as she drowned in her own blood. Her eyes closed, and her cold hands clutched at Jael's as shudders wracked her body. Then, incredibly, a smile touched her lips and the pain lines fled, leaving her face soft, peaceful.

Jael clutched her aunt's body close and held her, waiting, listening until she felt the last struggling beat of Modessa's heart. She stretched Modessa out and kneeled over her, trying to pray, keeping watch over her through the night as the woman's body cooled. She thought hard and long as she kept watch.

Jael knew she could not take Modessa's body home because her aunt's neighbors and fellow villagers would insist that she be buried according to their customs and not according to the rituals of the Hebrews. That would not be honoring Jehovah God. Jael decided that even though she could not follow the Israelites' customs, the intent of her heart would honor both her God and her aunt.

The next morning, she dug a deep grave for Modessa and prayed with many tears to Jehovah, the God of Israel. She vowed to her aunt that she would indeed follow the One True God. Then she laid Modessa down into the grave and placed a stone over it, rudely inscribed with the words: *Here lies Modessa, the Greatest Warrior this world has ever known.*

Full of grief and loneliness, young Jael returned home and found the fresh grave where her parents were buried. Grave offerings sat on a small altar before the spot, and she shuddered at the thought that her parents had never learned to love and serve Jehovah God.

Would she see them in the afterlife? Was there an afterlife? She would have to ask Joab if the Hebrews believed in an afterlife, as some of the Canaanite people did.

As she stood over their graves, remembering the past, someone touched her shoulder. It was Heber. He took Jael into his arms.

For the first time in her life, Jael allowed a man to embrace her. She thanked Heber for the loving burial of her parents. He comforted Jael and told her that he would take good care of her. Jael looked into Heber's eyes and knew he would someday be her husband.

In those days, it was said: *"A woman can see tomorrow, while yet a man is still searching for today."*

Because she couldn't stand to live in her parent's ravaged home, Jael decided to make Modessa's house her new home. Heber sent two of his best maids, Talmara and Asunda, to live with her and watch over her. He visited her often, bringing gifts, inquiring about her thoughts and feelings, and sometimes just coming to sit with her and watch the sunset or walk along the riverbank. His presence was a comfort to her.

As the days went by, love blossomed in her heart for Heber. She was not surprised when he sent intermediaries to her father's cousin, the nominal head of their family, to request that Jael be given to him as his wife. This cousin had always thought Jael was odd, being allowed to spend so much time with Modessa, and he agreed quickly, saying he was glad to no longer have responsibility for Jael.

Even while they were betrothed, Jael chose not to share with Heber her secret training and experience as a warrior. She never shared the grueling account of killing Zabed the Terrible and the painful burial of her Aunt Modessa. She would devote her whole life to being an excellent wife to Heber.

Unknown to Jael, her destiny was to become one of the greatest heroines of the Bible.

CHAPTER 4

A STRANGER IN THE NIGHT

It had been a very busy day for Jael. She and her two maidservants had cleaned every part of her house, washed all the dirty clothes, and fed all the animals.

Oh, I wish Modessa were still alive, Jael thought as she sat in her large bedroom, watching the sunset disappear. She missed her aunt and longed to see her parents again.

A year had passed since their deaths, yet she still felt hatred toward the men who rode with Zabed the Terrible. She couldn't hold back the tears that fell as she recalled her parents' horrible death at the hands of those savage beasts.

Well, Jael thought as she wiped the tears from her eyes, *life is very short, and tomorrow is not promised.*

Jael thought about her life. As a child, she had spent many hours with Modessa, becoming proficient in using various types of weapons and the deadly arts. She remembered Bezer the Bully, how God had used her at a young age to turn his life around, and the dangerous battle she had fought with Zabed the Terrible.

It was only with the help of the Lord that she had defeated him. She thought deeply about Modessa's last words to her, and tears flowed again as she thought of her great love for God.

"I love You, Lord, will all my heart and soul!" she exclaimed. "If I could just see you! You are so wonderful!"

As Jael stood in the middle of the room, she worshipped God. Fervently, she lifted her hands and gave thanks and praises to Him with a loud voice. She prayed for Heber, for she knew he served false gods. Suddenly, Jael realized she was not alone.

Even though it was nighttime, her room became brighter than the noonday sun. She looked into the brightness and beheld the most awesome features of a strange being. He looked like a man, yet he had two great wings. He stood with his head bowed down. He was a formidable sight, as one who had full authority over both Heaven and Earth.

Jael tried to scream for help from Talmara and Asunda, but could not utter a sound. She would have fainted, but somehow that too eluded her. Jael had no weapons nearby, and she knew within her spirit that this huge being could crush her with just one of his great wings.

The air was full of so much power and glory that it made all the skin of her body shiver and ripple, like a horse shuddering away from flies. She could even feel her hair standing upright on her head. She felt as though she weighed less than an eagle's feather and could take flight at that very moment.

Completely in awe, Jael looked upon him and saw that his two great wings seemed to be without end. Beneath his feet seemed to be rivers, oceans, nations of people, lightning, and great storms of all kinds.

His feet were as great as wheels, the size of two worlds, turning at a tremendous rate of speed, faster than the wheels of any chariot Jael had ever seen. Yet he stood still, with his eyes like flames of fire, staring directly at Jael. Then he closed his eyes. He seemed to stand higher than the clouds, yet he stood before her, seemingly about six cubits tall as a man.

Jael's heart beat dangerously faster than ever before as she realized that the being standing before her was not human. He was not of this world. Suddenly, he opened his great eyes again, and they burned like two vast furnaces of fire.

He opened his mouth and uttered words that had the sound of a trumpet. His words were not in her native tongue, yet somehow, Jael understood them.

His words were like rivers of many living waters of life flowing out of his mouth, sharper than any two-edged sword, saying, "Jael, my child, fear not, for I am the Angel of the Lord of Hosts, the Captain of the Armies of God. I come in peace."

"I am sent to you to anoint and strengthen you and tell you of things that will surely come to pass. Fear not, Jael, but fear the one who has sent me, whom you shall serve. You must fear Him always."

Suddenly, he reached out and touched Jael. Her knees immediately turned to water, and all of her breath seemed to leave her body, yet she lived. She fell down before him in worship.

Then he lifted her, and they seemed to become one. It was an intimacy Jael had never known, an ecstasy she had never dreamed possible, and yet it was holy, pure, and not of a sexual nature.

Astonished, Jael looked and saw a golden sash around his chest. His head and hair were white as the wool of lamb. Jael worshipped before him deeper, more fervently, on a higher plain than ever before, and yet she never uttered a word, neither breathed one breath of air into her body. Even though she didn't understand, in a moment, she transformed from finite to infinite and from humanity to divinity.

"Jael, my child," the angel said, "as I was with Moses, so shall I be with you. I was sent by the God of Abraham, Isaac, and Jacob, whom you now worship. God has chosen you as a choice vessel to be blessed above women and a conqueror for my people, Israel. Hear my voice, young Jael, and obey my words. I will be with you always, only be strong and of good courage."

"Your parents are with God, and Zabed the Terrible has been judged. As you go forth, I will lead and guide your footsteps all the days of your life, and you shall prosper and not be defeated. Behold, now I give you power and might above all of your enemies. God has anointed you for a purpose and has approved of Heber, your husband-to-be. Arise, Jael; take up your sword and shield. Go forth, for you shall deliver many from death."

It seemed that Jael opened her eyes that were already opened and looked upon the angel of the Lord. Suddenly, the angel disappeared, and Jael fainted.

Hours later, from the midst of the fainting darkness of sleep and visions, Jael heard a familiar voice calling her. It was Talmara.

"Jael! Jael! Are you all right?" She inquired.

"Yes, I am," Jael answered her.

"It is long past dawn," Talmara said, "and you are still in the house. This is not like you. Asunda and I were concerned. You always run far and practice with your weapons at dawn. Hurry, your breakfast is getting cold. You must come and eat."

"I shall be with you in a moment!" Jael said. Then she thought about the visitation of the Angel of the Lord. She bowed her head, saying, "Yes, Lord, not my will, but let Your will be done in my life."

As she stood up, Jael felt brand new. It seemed that the spiritual power of another source flowed throughout her entire body. Somehow, she just didn't feel as she felt before.

Her legs felt like iron, and her arms as great, powerful tree limbs. She knew she had been changed, and the anointing of God was now upon her life. She felt peace and a massive deliverance from the grief over the deaths of her parents and her Aunt Modessa.

As she sat eating her breakfast, little ripples of spiritual lightning seemed to run throughout her body. Suddenly, she was brought back to reality by Asunda's exclamation.

"Jael, that's enough! You must not eat anymore! It is important that you keep your beautiful figure for your husband. You are to be married in a fortnight," she scolded.

Jael laughed as she looked down at the empty platter of fresh bread and fruit. "This isn't like me at all!" She understood that her encounter with the Angel of the Lord had depleted her physical reserves, even though it energized her soul and spirit.

As Jael stood up and opened the door to go outside, she knew she had opened the door to a new pathway of life. Her destiny would be revealed, a future that no one knew but her God. With renewed faith, Jael boldly stepped out into the beautiful dawning of a brand new day.

THE WEDDING

Finally, the evening before the day of Jael's wedding to Heber arrived. Due to their divided beliefs and serving separate gods, they had agreed not to have a large wedding feast, but just a few friends, Talmara, Asunda, and Heber's family members.

Jael wanted Joab the Levite to speak blessings and offer the sacrifice at her wedding festival, but Heber wanted a traditional wedding with the priest of the local god he served and sacrifices for fertility and blessings on their wedding.

After much debate, they agreed that Heber would go to the temple to make the traditional sacrifices and then come to Jael's house to fetch her to his tent outside the city. Joab would pray over them before they left her house, asking for Jehovah's blessings on their marriage. To appease Heber's relatives and to protect Heber from mockery for letting his wife dictate their marriage from the start, the household idols would be present in their customary place of honor at the wedding feast.

Their love for each other was so great it would help them bridge many differences throughout their marriage, just as it had helped them find a middle ground in their marriage ritual and feast, Jael thought as she sat in her bedchamber. She loved Heber with all her heart. By tomorrow night, she would be known as Heber's wife. She smiled and let herself sink into dreams of a life with Heber and the many beautiful daughters and strong sons they would have together.

Suddenly, her quiet musing was shattered. Talmara gave a loud scream that filled the entire house and came running into Jael's room, her eyes wide with shock.

"Jael! Jael! Your dress for the wedding feast has been stolen! I washed it this afternoon and hung it on the bushes to dry. I was just going outside to bring it in when I heard horses. When I looked outside, I saw a woman snatch up your dress, leap on a horse, and ride away!"

Quickly, Jael dashed out of the house, hoping to apprehend the thief, but all she saw was a cloud of dust in the distance. Talmara said a woman had taken her dress. Above all evildoers, Jael despised a thief, especially a female thief.

Jael dashed into the room where she kept all her weapons and quickly armed herself. Then she ran to the stable and selected her best horse. As she leaped upon its back, a chill ran through her body.

Tears stained her eyes at the thought of not having that special dress for her wedding feast. Heber had insisted that she should wear purple, despite the expense of the dye, to signify to everyone the high value he placed on her as his bride. Jael cared more about Heber's disappointment and the fact that the dye had been a gift from him than the dress itself.

This woman thief would not succeed in marring her wedding feast! As fast as her stallion could take her, she rode into the deepening twilight after the departing thief.

ZALTURA THE THIEF

Zaltura was a large woman. She had been abducted from her home by Zabed the Terrible and was forced to be his mistress for the last five years.

She learned to love the barbarian, even though he was evil. He took good care of her and saw that all her needs were met. Zabed had promised to marry her someday.

She had grieved a long time after the men of Zabed's band of thieves and brutes brought back the news that two women had killed Zabed the Terrible and four of his best men. It was a dishonor to all men of war. She was pleased that Modessa was dead. With intense anger and hatred, she made plans for Jael's demise. Zaltura had bided her time to seek revenge upon Jael for her deeds.

"She will pay with her life!" Zaltura swore.

As time went by, she found out all she could about Jael. She found out where she lived and spied on her. She watched her for moons, learning her daily routine and habits. She employed two of Zabel's men to work closely with her, for she knew that any woman who could kill Zabed the Terrible could surely kill her too, even though she had slain a few men and women in her life.

Zaltura gave the town witch a large sum of money to find out Jael's weaknesses. Within a short time, the town witch reported that Jael's weakness was her hatred and fear of common rats and snakes.

When Jael was a child, some field mice had crawled into her crib and bit her several times. Since then, she had terrible dreams of giant rats chasing her while trying to eat her alive. Zaltura had thought about killing Heber but decided to set a trap to kill Jael with the help of hungry rats and her two hired ruffians.

As Jael's wedding day approached, Zaltura vowed that Jael would never live to know love or be embraced by the arms of a husband. Zaltura needed a way to lure Jael out of the house and into the woods. She waited for the perfect opportunity when no one seemed to be watching.

She gathered ten of the largest rats found in the woods, imprisoned them in a large water jar so they could not chew their way to freedom, and put them in the place where she and her men would set a trap for Jael.

Then she went to Jael's house and stole the expensive purple dress intended for her wedding. Then she rode as fast as she could to the place where her two ruffians awaited her return.

Zaltura looked at the beautiful dress in her arms, and with an evil smile of satisfaction, she said, "It won't be long; she will surely come." Her trap was set.

Jael rode hard after the thief. She slowed when she realized that she could still see the fleeing horse's tracks despite the thickening shadows of twilight and the surrounding woods.

As if the thief wanted her to follow her trail, out of nowhere, a shower of chittering, struggling, furious rats came flying through the air and landed on her and her horse. Terror and revulsion gripped Jael. Her horse screamed as the rats crawled over them, biting and clawing.

Jael screamed and flung her arms in the air, shaking off the rats. Her horse bucked and screamed as the rats clung to it, biting and clawing. Once again, Modessa's training struggled to the front of her thoughts.

Jael knew this was no accident: she had ridden straight into a trap. Faster than lightning, she drew her dagger and sword, shook off more rats that tried to crawl on top of her, and leaped from her horse to the ground. Maddened by rat bites, the horse made a dash for freedom, vanishing into the night.

A glimpse of movement causes Jael to turn, her dagger ready. She saw a man's shape and flung her knife, aiming for the heart. The man fell mortally wounded. Suddenly, a net spun through the air and opened wide as it flew over her. The stone weights tied to its edges brought it down on her before she realized what was happening.

The net's weight pinned her to the ground. Jael was helpless. Suddenly, Zaltura stood before Jael, tall, formidable, and full of wrath. She slapped Jael as hard as she could.

"You killed my beloved Zabed," she cried, "and now I shall kill you!" She drew her long sword to drive it into Jael's heart.

The other ruffian grabbed her arm, saying, "Zaltura! Not so fast! Jael is now helpless. Let's have some fun with her. She has dishonored you by killing Zabed, so let's dishonor her."

Zaltura was pleased at the thought of watching Jael being raped. She would prolong her enemy's torment, cutting off Jael's hands, toes, and ears before driving her dagger through her heart.

Zaltura put her foot on Jael's back to hold her down as the ruffian lifted the net and prepared to slip ropes around her hands to bind her. He forgot to remove his dagger before he got within reach of Jael's swift, clever hands. It cost him his life.

Jael saw the dagger and knew she had to get it if she would escape with her life tonight. She curled up, drawing her arms and legs close to her body.

Zaltura dug her heel into Jael's side and slapped her. The movement blocked the ruffian's view as he went down on one knee and leaned over Jael, trying to bind her hands. That was all the opening she needed.

She slipped the dagger from its sheath and twisted out from under Zaltura's foot before either realized what she had done. Zaltura staggered, thrown off balance.

Jael twisted and lunged from her knees, sliding the dagger home into the ruffian's heart. She yanked it free, slashed at his throat for good measure, then tumbled head over heels out of Zaltura's reach. The woman attempted to stab Jael with her dagger, but she quickly eluded her and disappeared behind a tree.

Something bit Jael's foot. It was one of Zaltura's rats. With one swing of the dagger, Jael quickly cut off the creature's head. She fought a shudder of revulsion and reached up her arms to climb the tree with a half-formed notion of dropping on Zaltura and knocking her unconscious.

Another shriek caught in Jael's throat as she looked up straight into the eyes of a huge snake. It was too dark to see anything but the snake's shape and the soft glimmer of light on its long fangs. Jael held still, not breathing.

Zaltura approached the tree, swearing and stomping. Her movements and body heat attracted the attention of the snake.

Jael darted back into the shadows as Zaltura came around the tree and stood directly under the snake. It dropped on her.

Jael held her breath, waiting, and jerked as Zaltura shrieked. The woman staggered away from the tree, her hands clawing at the bulk of the snake draped around her head and shoulders.

Jael didn't linger to make sure the snake killed Zaltura. Wisdom said to flee. She hated and feared snakes worse than rats. A few steps took her to the other side of the tree and through the bushes where the rats originally came from. Jael reasoned her stolen dress and possibly a horse to ride home would be in that direction.

Tears of relief and stressed laughter escaped her as she saw Zaltura's horse, tied on a bush, with her beautiful dress spilling out of a bag carelessly tied to the back of the saddle.

Jael left Zaltura and her henchmen to the care of the forest's beasts and headed home. She rode slowly, staying to the byways, avoiding the rough kind of men who would be active and roaming so late at night. The moon had started its descent from midnight by the time she reached her home.

Talmara and Asunda were nearly frantic with worry for her, but she was relieved to learn they hadn't sent for anyone, especially Heber, to search for her.

The two maids' questions faded to silence under Jael's stern expression and her refusal to answer any questions. They washed her rat bites and scrapes with wine and soothed them with oil, and left Jael to sleep through what remained of the night.

Asunda stayed up, washing and checking the dress for damage because Jael was to be married in the morning.

HEBER AND JAEL GET MARRIED

If beauty could express itself in words, it would write many books about the beautiful woman who waited inside her home for Heber to come fetch her. Joy glowed in her eyes as she met his gaze while the Levite, Joab, invoked blessings from the Israelites' god.

If handsome could speak, it would proclaim that the noblest man of the Kenites was Heber, a close relative of the king, wealthy in the metalwork trade and flocks. He proudly walked before the horse she rode as he led her to her new home in his tent.

Women going to the well in the morning cool and shepherdesses leading their flocks out to pasture stopped to stare at the man dressed in robes fit for a king, so handsome and filled with love for the woman of his dreams. The guests who waited at the tables set up outside Heber's tent saw how he looked at her as he helped her dismount, as if he looked at a goddess rather than a mortal woman.

"She is my diamond forever!" He exclaimed for all to hear.

Though the feast was small, Jael felt the presence of God. It comforted her as she looked around the feast and saw the statues of

Heber's household gods that surrounded the feasting square. She shuddered in disgust as various wedding guests stood up during the feast and offered prayers to the lifeless idols or poured out wine offerings to bring blessings of fertility to the newly married couple.

Jael silently prayed thanks again that Heber had agreed to her request not to bring those idols into their home. They would stay outside the tent in an encampment area designated for worship.

To win that agreement from Heber, Jael had agreed not to bring into their home the few precious scrolls of holy scriptures that Joab had given Modessa so many years ago. Just as Heber would worship his idols outside their home, Jael had arranged to have a small tent set up outside the encampment where she could worship in private and study the holy words of Jehovah.

Thinking back to that discussion with Heber, Jael smiled. Her husband had been stunned, almost speechless, to learn that his bride could read, write, and cipher like a temple-trained scribe.

She looked forward to many quiet evenings with Heber, teaching her beloved new husband to read and write for himself. He could cipher for the sake of his many business dealings, but this new talent would make him stand even taller among the Kenites and bring him honor. She was glad to bring that gift as part of her dowry to her beloved Heber.

At various times throughout the feast, Heber's attendants stood to offer toasts to bless the newly married couple. Each time, Heber and Jael joined hands and stood, accepting the acclaim of their guests.

After the second toast, Heber and Jael looked into each other's eyes, all the yesterdays fading away into tomorrow's promises. That moment held such love and passion that the air seemed to stand still. It was not necessary for anyone to breathe. Heber stood mesmerized, and Jael stood as in a hypnotic trance because the power and the presence of love were so great.

Jael did something that many would talk about for years to come. She let go of Heber's hand, lifted both of her hands, bowed her knees, and worshipped God with all of her heart and soul.

She cried out, "Hallelujah! Thanks be to God. Hallelujah!"

Even though it was a very radical act, no one murmured or complained. Suddenly, one after another, the household gods set up around the feasting square fell off the platforms they stood on. Only a few besides Jael and Heber noticed because most of the guests had their backs to the idols.

Heber stared, then turned to Jael, his eyes wide with wonder. Then he laughed, flung his arms around her, and kissed her in front of their guests.

As their lips touched, time seemed to stand still. Heber kissed a woman who was under the anointing of God, and he could feel the power of the spirit of God even upon her lips. It was simply awesome.

Heber felt his heart beat faster. His knees grew so weak and faint that he held on to Jael to keep from falling. Jael felt Heber's strength fading, and she knew she couldn't stand up on her own. Suddenly, she felt an invisible hand on her shoulder, giving her strength. Jael knew it was the hand of God.

That evening, as they entered their bridal chamber, she knew she gave Heber the key to her inner soul, the key to her heart that no man ever experienced. Heber picked up Jael and carried her into the bedchamber, where time ceased to exist. The night faded into noth-ingness, and even the creatures of the night seemed to stop their usual routine in honor of a great union.

CHAPTER 5

JAEL, BLESSED ABOVE WOMEN

J ael was a tall Kenite woman with extremely long, dark red hair and large brown eyes framed perfectly by long eyelashes. All who saw her agreed she was the most beautiful woman in the land.

She stood a head taller than all the women in the village where she had grown up and in the tent community outside the city of Hazor. Every stranger who looked upon her beauty described her as a goddess or a queen. However, the radiance of her lovely countenance could never match the inward beauty of her heart.

The name *Jael* (Goode, 2019)[1], which is of Hebrew origin (יָעֵל Yā ʿ ēl), means a mountain goat and one who ascends. Both the deer and the mountain goat depend entirely upon God, not man, for their sustenance.

Jael was a strong maiden, both mentally and physically. She was a precious noblewoman in her day. She was not a Hebrew, yet she believed in God. Jael walked with the God of the Hebrews and not the false gods of the land, air, and sea that most of the other Kenite women served.

She was a woman of great faith and highly respected in her community. Jael obeyed the laws of Israel and kept all the commandments of God. She obeyed the laws of Moses, to the dismay of many, especially her husband, Heber. She faithfully kept all the laws of the land as a woman of honor, respect, and humility.

Jael spent no time creating or spreading gossip, but always kept her hands busy. She was a knowledgeable woman, fashionable, and influential in decision-making when women gathered to discuss community matters. She was a woman of great virtue, style, kindness, and compassion.

Jael was God's jewel and Heber's diamond. If there was anything negative in her young life, it was the fact that she had no children, for she was barren. Many nights as she lay in her bed, she cried great tears for the sons she dearly longed for.

Jael's nomadic Kenite ancestry descended from Tubalcain. They were a wandering tribe associated intimately with the Midianites and the Amalekites. They lived in Canaan during the time of Abraham. During Israel's exodus from Egypt, the Kenites were there and showed kindness to Israel (1 Samuel 15:6, Nelson's Bible Illustrated Dictionary, 1986).

They were expert metal craftsmen. Moses' father-in-law, Jethro, was also called a Kenite (Judges 1:16). Some modern-day scholars suggest the skill in Israel's casting of the golden calf (Exodus 32) and the bronze serpent (Numbers 21) may have been learned from the Kenites, Jael's ancestors.

Ever since her childhood days of training with her Aunt Modessa, Jael loved to run long distances all by herself. It was one of her great pleasures and something she kept secret, even from Heber.

With the dazzling speed of an antelope, she would run in the early morning over the hills and valleys for miles. She loved the beauty of the great outdoors because she knew her God was there. She could feel God in the wind and see Him in the treetops.

She never forgot the time she ran for over six miles and stopped to drink at a wide, deep stream. As she gently kneeled down to drink, God called her name out of the midst of the water. She listened to hear His voice again as her heart pounded with joy. Then she jumped into the water, clothes and all, looking for God.

She wanted so much to see Him, touch Him, and know Him. The great love she had for her husband was nothing compared to the love she had for God. Once she married Heber, Jael's happiness was complete, except for one thing.

Many generations ago, armies from Egypt invaded Canaan and tried to conquer all the land to enslave the inhabitants to serve Pharoah. In honor of the victory over Egypt, a great competition was held in the spring before the first planting.

Each year, the New Moon Games were held at a different Canaanite city and lasted for many days. The festival included wrestling, feats of skill and speed and strength, and feasting. Warriors showed their battle prowess, and the fleetest runners proved their speed and endurance.

Women were not allowed to compete in the New Moon Games. Jael thought that rule was shameful because she knew no man at those games could beat her. Unfortunately, her Aunt Modessa's friends, who thought that women were the equal of men in intellect and skill, had no power in the councils of the various kings.

She tried speaking to Heber, hoping maybe he could convince the king of Hazor since they owned some allegiance to that Canaanite city. Heber spoke once to Jabin, but he never told Jael what the king's reaction was to his request. Jael could guess. The few times she was in Jabin's presence, the king sneered at her or spoke to the men standing around him, and they stared and laughed at her.

She vowed that someday, she would run in the New Moon Games and prove that women were indeed the equals of men and worthy of respect and consideration, just as her aunt and her scholarly friends had taught her.

One morning, Jael lay sound asleep in her bed when, suddenly, her dream was shattered by the sound of a large bird calling out in song for its mate, a sweet melody as loud as it could sing. She quickly sat up in bed, startled to realize she had overslept.

Yawning, she reached out her tender hands to awaken her beloved husband. To her surprise, she found Heber had left already. He told her the night before that he would leave in the morning to gather his men together. It was a time of declared war between Jabin, the king, and the people of Israel.

War is so very foolish, Jael thought. She slid out of bed and went to her knees to begin her morning worship. She prayed fervently to God three times each day since her conversion to Judaism. The beauty of her prayer was angelic. It may have gone something like this:

THE PRAYER OF JAEL

My Lord, Jehovah God, who created all things, I thank You for being so good to me. I thank You for all that You have done for me and my husband, Heber. I thank You for the great increase of our cattle and our land. I praise You that we have good health.

I praise You in advance, in faith, for my firstborn son, who will come someday from You, as you have shown me. Thank You for my awakening and for keeping my husband alive during the night.

Now, Heavenly Father, I thank You for another day. I ask You to use me as Your servant so that others may come to know You through me. Lord, help me to be a witness for You and a blessing to others. You have blessed me just as You blessed Father Abraham on the earth and from heaven above.

Help my husband to come to know You as I now know You. You are the one true God of heaven and earth who created all things by Your mighty power. Your grace and mercy are brand new each morning. Your love and kindness cover me, and in Your presence, I rejoice every day.

All praise, honor, and thanksgiving I give unto You. You are the strength of my being, and I am truly blessed. My Lord, help those who are poor, weak, and destitute who cannot help themselves. Heavenly Father, protect Your people Israel. Please have Your way, Jehovah God, in the wind, in the rain, and in my life, for there is none like You. Amen.

As Jael arose from her prayer, Deborah, the judge and prophetess, suddenly came into her mind. *Now there is a truly godly, anointed woman,* thought Jael. *I want to meet her. Someday I want to be just like her.* Jael had seen her as she led the Hebrew women in the worship services, but had never officially met her.

Jael prepared for her morning bath and to comb her long hair when suddenly she felt God's anointed presence. She sang songs of thanksgiving and deliverance to the Lord. She sang of His great mercy, goodness, blessings, and love for all mankind.

CHAPTER 6

DEBORAH THE PROPHETESS

(THE BEGINNING)

The book of Judges holds the story of Jael. Judges is a book about twelve male judges and one female judge. Deborah was a judge and prophetess who was mighty in her faith. Deborah was like the prophet Elijah; they both were blessed above.

After the death of Joshua, there was no one to lead Israel. Judges were chosen from the different tribes. Israel dwelt in the land of Canaan, the land of milk and honey. King Jabin had oppressed Israel for more than 20 years. God had given the Israelites over in Jabin's hand due to their rebelliousness, false gods, and many sins.

This is the same Canaan where Moses sent spies to investigate the land, namely Joshua and Caleb, along with ten others. They saw giants who were the children of Anak. Most of the spies were afraid; Joshua and Caleb were not. God gave the land to the Israelites.

After the death of Moses, Joshua became the leader of Israel. Israel served the one, true living God. After the death of Joshua, a new generation of Israelites rose up. They forsook God and served other gods of the people around them (Judges 2:10-19).

They served Baal and worshipped Ashtoreth. God's anger rose up against Israel and allowed their enemies to overtake them. Although they had judges who helped to deliver them, Israel refused to listen to the judges or obey the commandment of the Lord.

Israel was sorely vexed and daily oppressed. Later, they repented to the Lord because of their torment. Yet, ignorantly, they continued to serve other gods and break the law of Moses and the covenant of the true and living God.

Israel continued to be rebellious and stubborn. They forgot the Lord their God and served Baal and other idols (1 Samuel 12:9-11).

Several judges were sent by God to deliver Israel. The third judge, Shamgar, the son of Anath, slew 600 Philistines with an ox goad (a sharp metal point on the end of a long pole used by farmers to prod animals and keep them moving).

Even though Shamgar was a mighty man in strength, God chose a fourth judge, Deborah. She was God's mouthpiece, intimately acquainted and spiritually connected with God, and totally committed to serving Israel as God's servant. Her godly, anointed voice always demanded attention, and her prophetic words were beyond measure.

Deborah demanded great respect as a judge. During that time, a judge was almost equal to a king. Her husband, Lapidoth, was known in the gates, where men gathered together to settle personal issues. Being the first female judge, one can conclude that her name was known among all men, and she was the subject of both negative and positive conversation.

Deborah sat in judgment beneath the Palm Tree of Deborah, as it was commonly known (Judges 4:5). The Israelites received not only sound judgment from her but also divine prophecies of God. Deborah's name means *Speaking Bee* (Keegan Publications, 1990)[1], one who is eloquent and speaks as to him, one who sits among a swarm of bees and rules the beehive.

Being both eloquent and diligent, Deborah did all things in order, which is the nature of a bee. The name fits Deborah perfectly. Some scholars believe she chose the palm tree because it was considered a symbol of victory (John 12:13).

The Hebrew word for palm tree is the name of a woman, *Tamar*[2] (Genesis 38:6) and (2 Samuel 13:1). Deborah lived in the hill country of Ephraim between Bethel and Ramah. The palm tree where she judged was a very popular landmark for all of Israel.

No matter how well she judged, the people of Israel continued to do much evil in the sight of the Lord. Eventually, the Lord gave them over to King Jabin of Hazor. Sisera the Giant was the captain of his army.

The name Jabin means "he will understand (Abarim Publications)[3]." The name Sisera means "a field of battle[4]." Between the two of them, they understood the field of battle. Together, they were indestructible, or so it seemed.

These two evil men are mentioned in Psalm 83:9-10 (21KJV): "Do unto them as unto the Midianites: as to Sisera, as to Jabin, at the brook of Kishon, who perished at Endor; they became as dung, refuse for the earth."

It was a warm, fine, sunny day. Deborah was so tired, and the day wasn't even halfway over. She had judged six cases already. It seemed that the sins of Israel were still on the rise, and most of the men who came before her detested the fact that she was a woman judge.

Her thoughts were interrupted by several base fellows who approached swiftly, mounted on horses, determined to run her over.

She quickly stood and called aloud upon the name of the Lord. At the last moment, they turned away, and one man threw a folded document at her and fled away.

As soon as she opened the document, her greater fears were realized. It was a declaration of war from Jabin, King of Hazor, against the people of Israel. The war would take place within several days; the winner takes all.

"Many people will die. What are we going to do?" Deborah fell against the palm tree and laid prostrate upon her face before God. Tears flowed like a river down her face. She prayed to God with all of her heart.

THE PRAYER OF DEBORAH

Dear God of Israel, my Lord Jehovah, please hear the prayer of Your servant Deborah, whom You chose to rule and judge Your people, Israel. Hear my cry. I thank You for all that You have done for me in my life, especially for Your great salvation and tender mercies.

Heavenly Father, my King, I come unto You, for You know my needs even before I open my mouth. Your answer has already gone forth from Your presence. You know the document that has declared war against Your people, Israel, and I need an answer from You. You gave us this land of milk and honey. You blessed me through Your grace to have judgeship over Your people. I humble myself before You today. Should we flee for our lives, or should we stand and fight against impossible odds and Sisera, whom none has been able to defeat? I will do Your will, but I need to hear from You.

Deborah continued to pray, yet there was no answer. Hours later, she rose up with fear and confusion and went home in despair. What must she do?

While she had judged many cases with her people, the decision to fight or flee was far above anything she had faced. She entered her home in a daze, with the heavy weight of a decision upon her shoulders. She entered her prayer chamber and again spoke to the Lord in worship, prayer, and praise.

As she lifted her hands as high as she could, it suddenly appeared as if they were no longer a part of her body, nor was she in a human form. Deborah was caught up in His presence in the spirit with rapture, great joy, and peace. She tried to speak, but there came a divine voice from the throne room of the Most High, saying:

My child, fear not, for I am He. I am the God of your forefathers, the God of Abraham, Isaac, and Jacob. I have heard your cry; I have seen your tears. I call the ending forth before the beginning and things that are not in existence before time began. I have chosen you out of many generations to be a vessel of honor unto Me.

Who is he that can defy My will or destroy that which I have set for My purpose and glory? You must have faith. There is one among Israel named Barak, whom I have also chosen and anointed with you for greatness.

Hear me now, Deborah, and obey. I have made your name great, and it is written in the Book of Life forever. Do not fear the wicked Sisera, for my judgment is upon his life. I have called a woman out of the Kenite nation, one of great honor and stature, whom I love. She will destroy the wicked Sisera and deliver my people, Israel.

Now go call Barak and meet me at the Kishon River. I will be glorified during this battle. As I was with Moses, so shall I be with you. Prepare for me 10,000 soldiers. I will have honor over all of My enemies this day. Just as I did to Pharoah, I will eliminate Jabin from the face of the Earth, and he shall be no more. Go forth, dry your eyes, obey My voice, and live. I will fight for you. I am the Lord your God.

THE PROPHECY OF DEBORAH

Upon hearing the divine words of God, Deborah stood up and lifted her voice to the pinnacle of its power and prophesied until she fell asleep, exhausted. In the morning, she called for Barak and shared with him the word of the Lord.

There are some battles that we cannot win without God's manifested presence and the help of His mighty hands. Deborah's prophetic songs about this great battle are the only deliverance story in the book of Judges told poetically. The ending was known from the beginning.

Deborah's acclamation of Jael would be written in a song for all to see in the book of Revelations. It is one of the most magnificent works in the Old Testament. Like Jael, Deborah was blessed above women. She regarded Jael as her equal in spirit and compassion towards the work of God.

Deborah, a true prophetess in her time, prophesied the defeat of Sisera and Jabin before it came to pass. Both Deborah and Jael took their seats in destiny beside Elijah, Jeremiah, and Moses.

Jael's courage equals that of David as he faced the giant Goliath. Through a prophetic vision, Deborah knew that Jael, a non-Israelite woman, would perform a more daring feat than she or Barak and openly confessed, "Jael, you are blessed above women!"

Even though King Jabin oppressed Israel, Deborah had a vision from God that would sting both Jabin and Sisera to death in the end. She used her gift of prophecy. This mighty gift, used in conjunction with God's will and spoken by the prophet or prophetess, would bring to pass that which was spoken according to God's will, as He had shown them.

Deborah called to Barak and spoke by the power of her prophetic gift, by the will of God. She commanded Barak to gather 10,000 men of Israel to the Kishon River. There she would deliver the evil Sisera and his army of many thousands in Barak's hands.

Barak's name means "lightning and thunderbolt." His admiration of Deborah was very high, almost to adulation, for he said to Deborah: "If you will go with me, then I will go, but if you will not, then I shall not go."

Deborah, full of faith and a word from the Lord, said, "I will surely go with thee; notwithstanding the journey that shall not be for your honor, for the Lord shall sell Sisera into the hand of a woman," and Deborah arose and went with Barak to Kedesh (Judges 4:9, American KJV).

Moses told God exactly the same thing, saying, Lord, if you won't go with me, then I won't go (Exodus 33:12-15). God went with him.

Stunned by her words, Barak stared at Deborah in shock and disbelief. How could any woman stand up against the mighty Sisera when ten men would not dare to stand up against him?

Deborah said, "Rise up, Barak, let us go, for the Lord has already gone up before us."

At daybreak, the armies met. As Deborah and Barak sat upon their horses, viewing the vastness of the enemy, they heard the voice of Sisera giving the order to attack. By faith alone, Deborah lifted her hands to tell Barak to give the order for Israel's army to attack.

Sisera cried out to his thousands in a voice of thunder that seemed to shake the surrounding hills. "Attack! Attack! Attack!"

God fought for Israel.

Thunder rolled, the ground shook mightily, lightning came forth, and fire came down from heaven. The sky itself seemed to fall down from heaven. This was a true example to Israel and for us today, when God is on our side as we face insurmountable odds and our enemies outnumber us.

Immediately, the rain fell down like a river. The Kishon River quickly overflowed its banks. Sisera's army began to drown in the flood.

Later, Deborah and Barak would write songs about this great battle. They would tell their children's children how the stars fought against Sisera the Giant and Jabin the King. God sent heavy lightning and a downpour of rain that the Kishon River overflowed and flooded the plains where all of Sisera's chariots were.

The term *stars fought against Sisera* is not to be taken in a literal sense, but it is an indication of the futility of Sisera's fighting against God. Many times during our lives, when our backs are against a wall of trouble, stress, and danger, God will cause the source of our trouble more trouble so that we may be overcomers in victory!

Chariots of iron operate most effectively on flat, dry land. God turned the flat, dry land where Sisera's chariots were in the deep, muddy land by the overflowing of the Kishon River in Megiddo. Sisera's chariots and all of his army would perish, just as in the day when God brought Israel out of the land of Egypt when the waters flowed back across the Red Sea and all of Pharoah's army drowned.

On this day, only Sisera would remain alive to fulfill the prophetic voice of Deborah. God Himself would fight for His people. "Let God arise, let His enemies be scattered; let them also that hate Him flee before Him. As smoke is driven away, so drive them away; as wax melteth before the fire, so let the wicked perish at the presence of God (Psalm 68:1-2)."

CHAPTER 7

SISERA THE GIANT

Sisera, the captain of Jabin's army, was very happy. He had just received his instructions from King Jabin. Sisera was to gather his great army together and fight against Israel, whom he vehemently hated.

His instructions were to gather 900 chariots of iron and at least 26,000 soldiers of war to go up against Barak and the female judge at the Kishon River in Kedesh. He smiled, knowing Israel could gather no more than 10,000 soldiers, for he had oppressed Israel for over 20 years (Judges 4:3). But now it was war.

"Why are they so foolish?" Sisera thought out loud. "I could take just my 900 mighty chariots of iron and destroy them all!"

He was further pleased when the parchment letter from Jabin, the king, stated that he was to kill all the men of Israel and divide the spoils (wealth and women) among his men.

As the mastermind behind Jabin's successful army, Sisera sat down and drew up his plans of attack. He was familiar with the Kishon

River. He had hunted much game throughout his childhood and had caught much fish in the Kishon River.

"This plan is perfect. Israel, like all the others, does not stand a chance. Have they not learned that my name is Sisera, which means a field of battle? I believe I could kill over a thousand of those weaklings by myself," he boasted, as he flexed his biceps. No one had ever beaten him in a battle or hand-to-hand combat.

He was a giant of a man, standing well over five cubits tall: a burly, brutal, crude, and cunning man. Sisera was truly a belligerent military genius. He was arrogant and wealthy through thievery and deceit. He was antagonistic and sadistic; he dominated everyone like Canaanite dogs.

His mannerism was devilish. He was a rogue and a ruffian. Worst of all, a committed worshipper of Baal, he believed in sorcery and the occult. Some thought him to be a maniac, others a mercenary, and even some a manslayer who could show no sympathy. Satan himself enjoyed manipulating this wicked Sisera.

Sisera had no known father. His mother stayed young through magical enchantments, and it was rumored that she was the lover of Zalbazzar, the sorcerer.

By the time he was 12 years old, he had slain more than ten men in hand-to-hand combat. By the age of 20, Sisera had mastered many types of weapons. He was an expert in mortal combat and was extremely skillful in martial arts. He was also ambidextrous, able to use both hands with equal strength in battle.

Sisera's huge presence had a petrifying effect on any soldier. His height, weight, and heavy armor were awesome to behold. He was a monster of a man, a notorious, evil malefactor, arrogant and overbearing.

For over 20 years, Jabin used Sisera to persecute and oppress Israel. He was instrumental in the death of any. He raped many Hebrew women and killed a multitude of children. At age 40, he was a man obsessed with more power and authority.

He went into his tent, where a lifeless Baal stood alone. Sisera bowed down daily before his god, long before daybreak, to prepare for battle and what he thought would be the final slaughter of the Israelites.

Jabin is not worthy of being king, and I'm tired of just being a captain, Sisera thought as he left his tent. "I deserve to be king," he mumbled to himself. He knew his temporary position must not negate his predominant purpose to rule supreme as king.

With the help of Baal and Ashtoreth, he would surely rid the earth of all the Hebrews. Then he would easily attain the office of king, and his name would be the greatest in the regions. He was determined to bring all of his desires to fruition.

Sisera, in his evil mind, had a firm agenda. He would obliterate Israel's army and destroy their cities. He would save every young, beautiful woman for himself. The worthless old men and women would be killed, along with the young boys.

He would then kill Jabin in secret. Sisera would rule over his kingdom with a hand of iron. He would make war with all the surrounding cities in due time, conquering them all and taking them for his very own.

"The nerve of Barak and Deborah to insult me this way, coming before me in battle with only 10,000 weaklings," roared Sisera when his officers brought him news of the approaching army.

He arose and commanded his army of more than 26,000 men to move toward the Kishon River. 'This will surely be a slaughter today," he said to them all as he looked down upon Israel.

"We will all be back home before sundown," his second-in-command said. They both laughed.

Sisera raised his huge arms high, opened his mouth wide, and with a thunderous voice that shook the hills and valleys, he gave the order: "ATTACK! ATTACK! ATTACK!"

Little did he know that Jehovah God, the God of Israel, was looking down on him. God, in His mighty power, once again had prepared a flood. It would come to pass in the land of milk and honey that the mighty Sisera would be given milk to drink at the hands of a woman.

CHAPTER 8

JABIN THE KING

J abin, the King of Hazor, and four other kings sat upon their horses and watched from a distance. They all knew Israel's dismal army of 10,000 soldiers was as good as dead, with the mighty army of 26,000 advancing quickly toward them.

This will all be over quickly, Jabin thought. He had 6,000 soldiers, and the other four kings had come forth with 5,000 soldiers each. However, none of them knew the God of Israel never counted numbers, but He acknowledged the pure in heart.

None realized that man did not see as God saw. Man looked at the outward appearance, but God looked at the heart, and with Him, all things were possible.

Jabin, full of pride, thought about his kingdom, his 300 wives, and his concubines. He had all this at his disposal, yet he had never chosen a queen for his throne. He smiled as he watched Deborah.

Now she would be the perfect queen for me, Jabin thought. If only he could just force her to deny her God, Jehovah, to serve his gods, Baal and Ashtoreth. Two gods were better than one.

"Now there is a real woman," he said out loud. "A leader even among men, she would be perfect for my kingdom."

After the battle had been won, Jabin planned to order Sisera to kill all the Hebrews except Deborah and a few women who would serve as sex slaves for his soldiers.

Deborah's husband, Lapidoth, would be the first to die, and if she refused to become his queen, Jabin would burn her in the fire, and she would die a horrible death. He still didn't like the way Sisera looked at him lately, as though he was a piece of meat ready to be devoured. He would see to it that Sisera would never be king.

He smiled at the thought of forcing Deborah to be his queen. He asked himself: Could life get any better than this? Suddenly, his thoughts were interrupted by a loud crash of thunder.

Intense lightning seemed to hurl itself toward his army. Just as the two armies were about to engulf one another, the sky fell upon Jabin's army.

Hail, fire, and water came down like a flood, yet the sky was not cloudy. The earth trembled, and the mountain on which his chariot stood shook violently.

"What kind of sorcery is this?" The kings asked Jabin with much fear.

Immediately, the Kishon River overflowed its banks and became a raging river, flowing only toward Jabin's mighty army and the armies of the four kings. As if a giant had propelled the flood, thousands were immediately swept away (Judges 5:19-24).

Jabin knew the hand of the God of Israel was against him and moved against his troops. Jabin prayed fervently to his gods for help, and the other kings prayed to their gods, but none came to their rescue.

Within minutes, it was all over. All 26,000 perished except Sisera, who stared up at Jabin with horror and disbelief. Sisera was covered with mud and the blood of his own men.

"This is the work of the God of Israel named Jehovah!" Jabin shouted at the other four kings. "Run for your lives!"

Jabin looked back and saw Sisera fleeing towards Zaanaim and Barak, the captain of the army of Israel, in hot pursuit. Jabin and the four kings fled from the battle scene as Jabin began to plan.

He needed protection from Israel. His gods had failed him, and there were those who wanted his kingdom, even amongst the kings who were fleeing with him. In fear of Barak and Deborah, Jabin ran and hid in his chambers deep within his palace.

Seeing that the battle was now lost, Sisera quickly dismounted from his useless chariot of iron and threw down his weapons that had brought him success over the years. Infuriated and terrified for the first time in his life, he fled away on foot. The evil and mighty Sisera had only his feet in which to place his trust.

He felt no remorse at the loss of over 26,000 soldiers, just anger over the first battle he lost. He reasoned that he could always get other men to fight for him.

Just like Pharaoh, Sisera screamed and shouted obscenities as he helplessly watched the last of his army die within the floodwaters of the Kishon River. Their armor was just too heavy for them to swim. The water came down with such force that the rest of Sisera's army quickly perished.

We should have been able to slaughter Israel as planned, he thought.

Israel was greatly outnumbered. On that day, the God of Israel was just too strong. Sisera was puzzled, amazed, and shocked. He could not believe what had just happened. Even the skies seemed to turn into hail, fire, and water.

It did not rain a drop on Israel, but the flooding water seemed to chase after his army only. He had never seen anything like this in all of his days. He had seen many magical things the wizards had done, but the magic of Barak and Deborah was far too much for him that day.

Maybe there is a real God of Israel, he pondered, as a great fear of Barak came over him. Sisera, the cold-blooded animal of a man, calculated his options. One thing was certain: he must not allow himself to be captured.

FUTURE PLANS FOR SISERA, THE GIANT

Yes, I must live to fight another day, Sisera thought. *I must, and I will succeed! But why did my gods fail me? The gods should have given me a warning! I must perform a three-day ritual for my gods and then hear what they say to me. I am sure Baal and Ashtoreth are not pleased with this loss. Maybe I should look for another god.* [Just before he cut off the head of an Israelite mother, she told him that her God was the true and living God of Israel, a God who could do the impossible.]

Suddenly, he looked into the distance and saw a man running toward him. Stunned, Sisera fled for his life. He knew his gods were not with him. He knew by the size and speed of the man running toward him that it was Barak, the captain of Israel's army.

Sisera realized that if the God of Israel had power over heaven and earth, that same God would fight against him. If he turned and tried to slay Barak, he would surely die.

Sisera ran away with all of his might. He would rebuild an army more powerful than this one. He would kill all the Israelites: every man, woman, child, and even the old men. He vowed not one Hebrew would be left in the nation.

Next time, he would surely bring his gods along with him to fight their God and destroy Israel. Also, he would consult the mediums and soothsayers in the temple of his gods, especially Zalbazzar, the dark and fearful sorcerer. He would have them cast a spell on the God of Israel, for he had underestimated the power of the God of Israel.

Sisera dared not go to his mother's house to hide from Barak. His enemy would surely look for him there. He fled like a madman, full of rage, bitterness, and anger. Instead of panicking, Sisera sought a place of refuge.

He remembered a Kenite named Heber, and his wife, Jael, who lived in the tent community outside the city. They were friendly to Jabin. No one would suspect he would go there. Heber's tent was the only place in the area where Jabin was not hated.

Howbeit, Sisera fled away on his feet to the tent of Jael, Heber's wife, for there was peace between Jabin, the king of Hazor, and the house of Heber (Judges 4:17). Unknowingly, Sisera ran to his doom when he ran to the tent of the mighty female warrior, Jael. Now he was very thirsty and tired.

After he had rested, he would kill Barak, who was chasing after him. He would relish taking off Barak's head with one great swing of a mighty sword, just as he had done many times before to hundreds of other men.

He would also kill Jabin, the king, and pronounce himself the king of Hazor. None would dare come against him. Most of all, he would surely burn Deborah, the prophetess, as an offering to Baal.

I bet she would really prophesy then, Sisera thought as he smiled, showing a half-full mouth of missing teeth. They all would pay for this day.

He would retaliate with great revenge over all those responsible for this great loss in the day's battle. He would crush all of Israel under his feet once and for all. There would be no resistance. The God of Israel would surely learn to reverence his gods.

This loss was embarrassing and ridiculous. Sisera had warned Jabin about that woman judge. He felt that she was not normal, but Jabin disagreed, thinking she was "just a woman."

Israel allowed a woman to judge them; they deserved to die, showing just how weak they were. Oh, how wrong he was, and for this, Jabin the king must surely die. Sisera would be king and no one could ever stop him.

Sisera ran faster toward Jael's tent. He did not know that Jael was God's advocate, His deliverer for Israel, or that God had given her a divine assignment concerning him. In his wicked mind and black heart, Sisera could not perceive that what God had spoken of no man could change.

Staggering and shattered, he headed for the door of Jael's tent, which was pitched outside the city of Ziaam. He thought he would find safety within, yet, unbeknownst to him, he approached death's door.

One would think that Jael was a poor nomadic woman since she lived in a tent, but Abraham, Isaac, and Jacob all lived in tents. They were all very wealthy men, blessed above by God.

The fact that Heber was in alliance with Jabin and Israel indicated that Heber was a man of high stature and had much favor in the local community. Also, the kings in those days did not associate themselves with common people. The scriptures tell us that King Jabin was at peace with Heber, Jael's husband (Judges 4:17).

According to the Jones Dictionary (Keegan, 1990[1]), "Heber" means a "society, a company, or a charmer." In biblical times, names were given to match the personality and character of a person. Therefore, Heber was a society or a company of people.

By his charming power, Heber had charmed King Jabin, and Sisera knew of their peace. It is more than likely that Heber was a wealthy and influential man because of his metal working trade–including weapons of war–and his flocks. Jabin would only be acting wisely to be on friendly terms with him for the sake of politics.

God knew Jael's heart and the great inward riches she possessed. Deborah's affirmation of Jael spoke of her great character, honor, virtue, and wisdom. Jael's pure heart, wisdom, and understanding made her God's divine choice.

Although Jael was not a Hebrew, she was a chosen vessel of God, proving that the color of one's skin, wealth, or popularity does not really matter, but only the condition of one's heart. Jael was a willing servant, highly favored, and truly blessed above women.

God revealed to Deborah the prophetess, by visitation or vision, that Jael would slay Sisera, and she would surely deliver His people. Deborah spoke of God's divine warrant and the execution of Sisera into destiny, and both were to be fulfilled by Jael. Unknown to man, this is the statement written by the finger of God and sealed in the Spirit Realm:

"Sisera, thou child of Satan, just as you thought to destroy My people Israel this day, you yourself shall be destroyed by an iron nail and a hammer at the hands of a woman."

CHAPTER 9
JAEL THE CONQUEROR

Blessed above women shall Jael, the wife of Heber, the Kenite, be blessed shall she be above women in the tent (Judges 5:24).

Jael worshipped God more frequently that day, as she knew the battle lines were drawn. After prayer and fasting, her morning solemnity was shattered by the sound of feet running toward her tent.

Then she heard a harsh voice commanding her to open the tent door. A chill ran down Jael's spine. Heber had gone early that morning with his men to deliver orders of weapons and chariots. Could something have happened to him between the battlefield and returning home? Why hadn't he returned home?

Agitated and fearful, she ran quickly toward the door, expecting to see one of her husband's servants and hear him deliver bad news. When she untied the door and looked out, she received the shock of her life.

The dirty, bloody, armored brute of a man could only be the wicked Sisera, whom all of Israel feared so much. She remembered seeing him from a distance as he talked with Jabin and her husband. He stank of death, mud, blood, and fear, his teeth bared as her, his eyes wide open. Was that terror in his eyes?

It struck Jael at that moment that this wasn't a victorious brute, drunk with victory and ready to pillage and rape the surrounding countryside, whether the people in his path were allies or enemies. This man was afraid.

She nearly smiled and laughed aloud as she realized there was only one answer—the God of Israel had risen and fought in defense of His people, just like in the old tales Joab the Levite told her when she was a child.

At that moment, Jael remembered something her Aunt Modessa and her warrior friends had taught her: A wounded, cornered animal is the most dangerous of all, and a defeated soldier is the worst kind of wounded, cornered animal.

She was alone today. All the male servants were with Heber. All the female servants were at the river, washing clothes or tending the flocks, or had walked to Ziaam to tend to various errands.

Jael had planned to spend a few quiet, precious hours studying a new scroll of scripture Joab had loaned to her. Instead, her spirit cried out in frantic prayer to the God of Israel because the filthy, terrified, and brutal enemy of His people had come to her tent.

There was no one to help her but Jehovah God. Her weapons were far away, hidden from sight. Before she could flee to another portion of the main tent and retrieve even a small cooking knife to defend herself, Sisera would be on her.

The best way to keep a lion from chasing you, Aunt Modessa had once told her, is not to run.

Jael quickly composed herself and put on her best welcoming smile. She had never felt so helpless and alone, realizing what a fool she had been to put on so much faith in her sword and dagger, spear and bow. Her life was now in serious danger.

This was an unexpected test of her faith, a demon attack of the spirit of fear. It was also a trial that no other woman in her time had ever experienced. Jael's miracle was in the midst of her problem, yet she could not be victorious until God's purpose was fulfilled in her life.

Sisera sagged against the post that supported the doorway of the tent of Heber, still gasping for breath after running such a distance in full armor. With a hiding place only a few steps away, his normal lecherous nature rose again. All he saw before him was a slim, beautiful woman with no one else in sight. Lonely, beautiful women were his favorite prey.

He leaned closer and was delighted when she stepped back into her tent. He mistook her disgust at his smell for fear and automatically relegated her to the category of easy victim. He quickly surveyed her tent, satisfied that she was indeed all alone and defenseless.

Yet he was bewildered by her lack of fear. That made him angry. People who made him angry had to be punished.

Common sense told him it was foolish to lash out at this woman when he was tired and famished. She would try to run away, and he was too tired to chase a silly woman.

He would make her serve him and give him shelter and food before punishing her. He would rest there until Barak passed by. Then he would rape Jael before killing her. For sport and to soothe his soul over the painful defeat his army had suffered, he might just wait for her husband to return home and kill him, too.

Still, he was amazed that his size did not completely intimidate Jael as he had hoped. Most women fainted at this presence. Sisera scowled deeper and glared harder at Jael, then bared his teeth. The entire confrontation took only a few heartbeats as each assessed the other from opposite sides of the tent doorway.

Jael silently prayed to Jehovah God, and a sense of peace descended on her. She looked deep into Sisera's face, even into his glaring eyes, and detected deep fear and consternation.

He is afraid of something or someone, she thought. Before she could utter a word, God spoke to Jael at that very moment in a still, small, and soothing voice. While it seemed like a long conversation, in reality, it was no more than a few seconds.

GOD SPEAKS TO JAEL

Jael, my servant, blessed above women! Standing before you is the wicked and evil Sisera. My enemy and your enemy, the most evil one upon the face of the earth. Fear him not, Jael, for I have delivered him into your hands. As I was with Moses and Joshua, so shall I be with you this day.

Obey My voice, and you shall live, for I have chosen you to be My deliverer, even a champion for My people Israel. For this cause, you were born. This evil Sisera has slain many innocent people of Israel—men, women, and children. Only be strong, Jael, and be of good courage.

Prepare to rise up and slay him, for My prophetic word has gone forth from My mouth to My servant, Deborah, the prophetess, and My word must be fulfilled. I will make your name great; even place your name in the Lamb's Book of Life.

All men, from the least to the greatest, shall speak and sing of you and shall call you blessed above all women. They shall sing of your mighty deeds and read in many books of your great work for Israel on this day.

And yes, you shall bear many sons for Me, and I will be with your seed forever. Behold, I have heard all your prayers and have now put my spirit upon you. Only be strong, for this Sisera is surely worthy of death. You shall know that I am with you when he asks for water to drink. But do not give water, give milk, and then he shall fall into a deep sleep. My presence shall go with you.

Have faith, Jael; be of good courage, for you shall find the weapons you need lying within reach of your tent. Now, rise up and slay him, as I have commanded you. Let him come in. Behold, I have spoken; now is the appointed time.

Jael knew the words spoken to her were infallible and came forth from the Almighty, infinite God, Jehovah.

Yes, my Lord, Jael said within herself. *I shall obey and deliver Israel from this evil Sisera.*

She blinked and took a step backward into the tent. Sisera followed her, repeating his demands that he be allowed into the tent.

Only a few more heartbeats had passed, though Jael's world seemed to have changed in that fraction of time. She knew that she could not deviate from God's strict instructions and divine assignment. With a hospitable attitude, an accommodating voice, and a smile, she answered Sisera.

"Turn in, my lord; please do not fear. You are welcome here!" Ever so nimbly, with the daring of a lion, she took hold of Sisera's hand and spoke politely again. "Do come in. You must be famished."

Sisera smiled and lost his fear at the most welcomed invitation he had ever heard. This woman had called him "Lord" with a smile. He looked around the tent, his greedy soul immediately considering the possibility of making the contents of the tent—especially the woman —his possession. It would be a crime, after all, to kill a beautiful woman who knew him and smiled at him, without beating her first.

As Sisera entered her tent, Jael, the tender Kenite woman, became a warrior, stepping toward her divine destiny. She knew she must be very careful, cunning and yet remain calm. She could not dismiss the possibility of her husband's return.

Sisera, like so many men, considered her weak and helpless simply because she was a woman, and he had visibly lowered his guard. As long as she stroked his pride and made much of him, he would be as harmless as a lamb.

But the moment a man entered the tent, he would become dangerous. She obeyed the voice of God, even though she realized her life, maybe even Heber's life, was in the balance.

The very thought of killing anyone again made her nauseous and nervous. Another chill ran down her spine as she watched Sisera straighten his shoulders and saunter around the main living area of the tent.

Jael watched as he surveyed every item: the low, round table with its display of bowls and cups with their intricate glazed designs that had been wedding presents; the brazier full of banked coals, and the circle of cushions around it where guests sat, talked, and ate; and the other furnishings of the tent that made it a lovely, comfortable, and welcoming place for friends and guests.

Skins of wine and milk hung on the tent posts, ready to be served to guests. Fruit, bread, and cheese waited in covered containers for the ready hospitality expected of the people of this territory.

Jael looked at her home with new eyes and realized that what she saw as comfortable and pleasing, someone else would see only as a sign of riches to be plundered. What did Sisera see now and plan to take with him when he left? She knew his reputation as a brute and bully, taking whatever he wanted, beating and even killing those who dared to protest.

Then Sisera turned and looked her over again, and the tight line of fear and tension around his mouth relaxed even more. She knew what Sisera planned to take while he was in the tent and wondered why he hadn't yet followed custom and asked about her husband.

Was he that certain of his superior strength and his success in taking what he wanted that he didn't care where her husband was or when he would return? Or did he know something about Heber that she hadn't heard yet?

It struck her again that she was all alone in this—alone with Jehovah God to guide and strengthen her and give her courage.

This was Jael's climactic moment. She knew her destiny would ultimately be fulfilled in the divine purpose of God.

Jael's actions would not just determine the fate of her own household, but of all of Israel. There was no escape. Her back was against the wall.

Just like Eve when she faced the devil, Jael felt trapped in a snare. Yet, unlike Eve, she saw her problem as a great opportunity to obey God.

Jael knew that Sisera was trained in war and hand-to-hand combat. No man could ascend to the high position of commanding Jabin's army without conquering many strong men. Even though she was far outweighed by his physical strength and outmatched by his training, Jael used her inward weapons of kindness, humility, wisdom, and virtue, which were far better weapons than physical strength.

Sisera only saw an empty tent and a weaponless young wife, but he never saw the great two-edged sword in Jael's mouth and the great dagger and spear of her character and divine appointment. Sisera became a piece of clay in the hands of a Master Potter. Sisera saw Jael as helpless and completely unarmed.

In truth, Jael was anointed, chosen, and fully armed with many weapons within her spirit, mind, and soul, especially the great weapon of obedience to God. With a small, harmless voice, Jael put the evil mind of Sisera to rest. She became the avenger instead of the planned victim. She became Jael the Conqueror.

JAEL SLAYS SISERA THE GIANT

Truly, this confrontation between Jael and Sisera was a pre-David and Goliath occurrence. Jael continued to encourage and strengthen herself in the Lord. While Sisera was King Jabin's hero, Jael was God's heroine.

Just as God had told her He would do, Sisera looked down upon Jael with a contemptuous attitude and raspy voice, saying, "Give me a little water to drink, for I am very thirsty."

Quickly and carefully, she opened a fresh skin of milk and poured it into her most beautiful pitcher to serve it and the largest, most elaborately decorated cup for him to drink from.

Jael's demeanor was soothing and harmless. Her soft, meek voice was like a balm to the brutal Sisera.

As Jael, God's executioner, watched Sisera drink large quantities of milk, she studied him, noting his huge muscles, the weapon still strapped to his side and the armor that would protect him from her fists and nails. Jael knew that after Sisera had rested, he would do her bodily harm, either simply taking his pleasure in rape and robbery or killing her.

Well, she thought, *he shall not get the opportunity!* She pampered and coaxed him in the midst of her perilous situation, urging him to drink more, offering soft cushions to lie down, and flattering his soldier's physique.

Sisera became very sleepy under Jael's soothing, soft, tactful tone of voice. He thought in his heart, *Maybe when I awake, I will just kill her husband and take Jael to be my queen after I become king.*

Jael's character overwhelmed Sisera's common sense. He failed to realize that spoken words were more powerful than physical strength.

With comforting words, she coaxed Sisera to lie down. She gently covered him with her best blanket to make him feel comfortable and more at ease. Her life was still in jeopardy, so she could not allow Sisera to become cognizant of what was now in her heart.

Jael no longer felt intimidated as she took inventory of her only weapons at hand: a huge tent peg and mallet, which one of the servants had left in plain view after tending to his morning chores of checking the tent braces, pegs, and cords.

Jael thought the men had probably been in such a hurry to leave with Heber so early that morning that he had been unable to put away his tools as usual. She thanked Jehovah God for that carelessness.

Cursing and swearing, despite his exhaustion that made his words slur and his head heavy, Sisera ordered Jael to lie. "If anyone comes to the tent asking if you have seen me, you must tell them no." With much confidence, Sisera fell into a deep sleep, affected by the milk Jael had fed him.

Slowly and quietly, Jael went over to where the tent peg and mallet lay. With her left hand, she grasped the peg, and with her right hand, she lifted the mallet.

She was changed from a kind, gentle, loving, and tender Kenite wife into a warrior, an executioner, a mercenary, and a conqueror without mercy. For just a moment, she stood motionless as a lioness, poised to strike.

I must not fail God, my family, or Israel, she thought. As she placed the pointed end on Sisera's wide temple, Jael felt the anointing power of God as never before.

In one fluid motion, with all her strength of body and spirit, she struck the head of the peg with the mallet. It was a powerful, deadly blow.

Sparks flew as Jael drove the peg with great force. The sound of metal exploding against metal penetrated the tent's walls and was heard a far distance away. The Bible states in Judges 4:21 that the nail (peg) went completely through Sisera's forehead and fastened itself deep in the ground.

Jael's tent was a place of blessing. Sisera was cursed. No curse may stand or rest in the presence of the blessed above.

In Jael's time, what a woman possessed in her tent determined her overall status among women. Jael's hunger and thirst to please God and her commitment to obey Him were greater than her fear of Sisera. The fact that Jael was blessed above women meant that she had much wealth and many items in her tent of great value.

A mallet and tent peg, common everyday tools, had become the most valuable items in the tent. Most assuredly, there are things in our lives we often see as being of little value, yet they become priceless in a time of need.

Jael was a very astute woman. She was the only woman in the scriptures whose great character and virtue were described by another woman, Deborah, whom she had never met. Like Jael, every believer should be prepared to kill if they are in God's will, especially targeting the enemy who comes to steal, kill, and destroy.

Jael used the only available weapon to fulfill the will of God. She delivered everyone in danger of Sisera's plans, including herself.

Notice how Jael was blessed above women, and she heard from God. God knew Jael, even though she was not an Israelite, was willing to do everything God had told her to do. This is the same spirit that rested on David as he took his slingshot and drove a stone through the forehead of Goliath. God could have killed Sisera along with his army, but he spared Sisera for Jael.

Jael never let God down. This is the supreme example of the meaning of obedience and courage with faith.

Like Christ, Jael had been given divine instructions and was willing to sacrifice her very own life. She never looked at the power of the enemy against her, but put faith in God. She was not blessed above women just because she killed Sisera but also because her daily lifestyle and heart were a blessing to God.

God wants us to be a blessing to Him, as He is a blessing to us. We bless God when we do His will. Jael executed God's will. This was accomplished when she received the plan, the purpose, and a word from God. Then she said, "Yes, God," and obeyed His command.

Jael acted with such humility and kindness that it caused Sisera to have complete trust in her, and he fell asleep. We know that we are blessed above when our enemies, by our demeanor and conversation, have complete trust in us. Even though some may see Jael's actions as murder, God did not because she had received a divine assignment from the Lord.

Most definitely, we need more Jaels in our Christian society today, great women and men of God who are not afraid to do God's will in difficult or adverse circumstances.

Jael's courage and faith matched Daniel in the lion's den; David as he stood before Goliath; Rahab as she hid the spies of Israel in her home; the Hebrew boys as they faced the fiery furnace; and Ruth as she worked hard in the fields and was confirmed by Boaz to be a virtuous woman.

"And now, my daughter, fear not; I will do to thee all that thou requires: for all the city of my people doth know that thou art a virtuous woman (Ruth 3:11)."

Traditionally, a woman was not to go to battle to fight in a war and kill men or be killed by men. But man sees not as God sees, nor thinks as He thinks.

Man still looks at the outward appearance, but God looks at the heart (1 Samuel 16:7). God's choice was Jael. He uses the most blessed vessel that is inwardly prepared to do His will from the heart (Ephesians 6:5-6).

CHAPTER 10
BARAK MEETS JAEL

S isera's mother lived in the same area as Jael. In fact, we see in Judges 5:28 that Sisera's mother was looking for him to come to her house. "The mother of Sisera looked out a window, and cried through the lattice, Why is his chariot so long in coming? Why tarry the wheels of his chariots (Judges 5:28)?"

The first place Barak would have thought to look for Sisera would have been in his mother's house, but Sisera did not go there. Barak was still hotly pursuing Sisera and now approached Jael's tent. Meanwhile, Jael looked down on Sisera as he lay lifeless on her tent floor.

Slowly, Jael dropped the mallet, her weapon of destruction. She bowed her head and fell to her knees in prayer. She asked God for His forgiveness and mercy if He was not pleased with the brutal way that she killed Sisera.

Once again, a small voice came forth from the infinite throne of mercy, saying, "In you, I am well pleased."

Encouraged, Jael lifted her head. Common sense said someone had been chasing Sisera after the defeat of his army. She stood up and went boldly out of her tent to wait for whoever would come from the army of Israel.

Meanwhile, Barak was frustrated and still somewhat desperate. He did not know where the evil Sisera had gone.

"A defeated animal-like Sisera has the power to slay a hundred people," Barak said to himself. He drove his chariot as fast as the horses could carry him. Sisera eluded him on foot, nonetheless. He approached the territory of Zaanaim, where a community of Kenites had pitched their tents near Hazor.

Barak shuddered at the thought of Sisera stopping to wreak havoc on the peaceful metalworkers and shepherds who lived in those tents. Could Sisera be foolish enough to waste time harming innocent people before finding shelter in his mother's home (his mother who was reputed to be a sorcerer's lover)?

From the corner of his eye, he saw movement. A woman waved her arms, gesturing for him to come to her tent. Barak guided his chariot toward her. Common sense said to head into the city, but that quiet, wordless voice that had been guiding him since Deborah spoke her prophecy now urged him to see what this woman wanted.

As he drew closer, the realization penetrated his exhaustion and battle soreness, and desperate need to find Sisera that the most beautiful woman he had ever seen stood before him.

"Who are you? Whose tent is this?" Barak asked, stopping his horses. He staggered a little as he bent his legs to step down from the chariot.

Please, great Yahweh, God of Israel, let our enemy already be defeated and let Israel be safe once again, Barak thought as he approached Jael.

"Can I help you? Are you in need of help?" Barak asked.

"Welcome. I am Jael, wife of Heber, a noble of the Kenites, and these are our tents." She gestured at the cluster of tents spread out behind the large main tent, where she stood in the doorway.

"You are an Israelite soldier, yes?"

"I am Barak, commander of the armies of Israel and of Jehovah God." He pressed his fist against his dirty breastplate in salute to her.

"You seek Sisera, commander of the armies of Hazor, and King Jabin?"

Barak stared at Jael, stunned to hear that name in her warm, musical voice. A jolt of fear on her behalf shot through him. The thought of such a woman being threatened, much less harmed by a beast like Sisera, made him ill. He wanted to stand between her and any danger that might threaten.

Idiot! He scolded himself as he took a few steps closer to her. She is the wife of another. You can't be half in love with her so quickly.

"Yes, I hunt Sisera. Have you seen him or heard word of where he went after the battle? Don't be afraid – his army was destroyed, and he is a man alone. He will soon be hunted down and defeated."

To his utter surprise, she replied, "Yes, of course, I have seen him. Barak, commander of the army of Israel, servant of the Most High God, I will show you where your enemy lies. Surely he shall not trouble you or Israel anymore."

Barak nearly staggered as Jael gestured for him to follow her into the tent. Sisera was in her tent? How had she escaped rape and murder?

Quickly, he drew his sword. As he entered Jael's tent, that wordless voice of guidance from the Lord grew stronger within him. Then he realized that sense was not within him but filled the tent. His knees tried to fold for a moment as he realized he could feel the presence of God.

Yet he could also detect the presence of death in the air. Then he saw Sisera's body, and the impossible became a reality. His mouth dropped wide open.

He stared in shock and utter surprise. Evil Sisera lay dead on the floor with a tent nail driven completely through his forehead. Just as Deborah had prophesied, Sisera lay slain upon the tent's floor, killed by a woman.

Barak fell to his knees before Jael, speechless, with tears of gratitude flowing from his eyes. He took hold of her tender hands that held great strength and kissed them several times. Looking up into her eyes, he knew what he saw there was pure and divine.

Sisera never stood a chance against this most beautiful of weapons in the Lord God's hands, Barak thought. *Jael, truly you are blessed above women*, he vowed, his heart and voice overflowing with respect and awe.

Jael smiled. "To God be the glory, for it was He who anointed me and chose me to be a deliverer for Israel today. The Lord's will must be done. I am but a vessel chosen for the Master's use. It is He whom I serve. The God of Israel, the God of Abraham, Isaac, and Jacob, showed me how to defeat this evil Sisera. Therefore, I thank Him and give Him all the glory, honor, and praise."

Again Barak was shocked. With household idols standing in the open space in front of her tent, this Kenite woman served the Lord Jehovah, the God of Israel. Barak felt humbled before Jael, as one is humbled in the presence of royalty. His heart was in her hands.

His need to defend her turned to adoration. Combined with her great beauty, wisdom, and servant's heart devoted to Jehovah God, she was his ideal woman. Yet she belonged to another man.

Barak knew he must leave before he told her of his growing love for her. He kissed both her hands, lingering on the soft skin that hid such strength. Then he released her hands and stood.

It took all his strength of will not to clasp her shoulders and hold her still so he could look down into her eyes and feast on her beauty until his soul and spirit were renewed.

Jael shivered, seeing something new in Barak's eyes. What startled her was that the emotions and hunger she saw were familiar. That was the look of adoration Heber cast on her. Only Heber had ever looked at her that way when other men watched her with lust and the greed of someone wanting to possess a treasure. Why would Barak look at her as her husband did? Could his heart be turned toward her?

Her Aunt Modessa had told her of the strangeness that settled on the hearts and minds of men and women after a battle or a great catastrophe when death came perilously close, and lives were saved only after great pain, risk, and courage. Jael told herself that Barak suffered from that strangeness.

After all, he had been in battle today and was shocked to find his brutal, giant enemy slain. When he had time to wash, rest, and eat, his mind and heart would return to normal.

The important thing was to get Sisera out of her tent. Perhaps it was even more important to get him out of her tent than it was to get Barak to leave before Heber returned.

"We need to remove Sisera from my tent," Jael gestured with a shaking hand at the blood, and Sisera's brains spilled on the floor of her tent.

"I can cover the hole, but I don't know if I can remove the stain before my husband returns. I do not know what I can say to explain this to him."

"Tell him the truth," Barak said, taking a step back. To her relief, that strange warmth, hunger, and adoration were already fading from his eyes.

"Tell him that Yahweh, the God of Israel, has done mighty things for His people Israel, and you have been blessed to be a weapon in the One True God's hands." He bowed to her, saluting her as a soldier salutes a king, then dropped to his knees and grasped the end of the tent peg with both hands to pull it out of Sisera's skull.

Together, they dragged Sisera's filthy, heavy body out of her tent and loaded it into Barak's war chariot. There was barely room for him to stand.

By this time, many people had gathered around Jael's tent due to the presence of Barak's chariot sitting so long in front of it. When they saw Sisera's dead body, every soul stared in awe and unbelief.

Barak and Jael lifted the giant Sisera into the chariot. Unknown to them, two evil spies, servants of Adah and Sisera's mother, were in the crowd.

As Barak quickly rode away with Sisera's body, he thought, *I can hardly wait to see the look on Deborah's face when she hears how her prophetic word has come to pass, just as God has shown her.* He thought about Jael, whom he now cherished, and Deborah, whom he honored and served. He said within his heart that both of them were most certainly blessed above women.

Again Barak looked down upon Sisera, lying dead at his feet in his chariot, with awe and unbelief. As he came towards his army, hundreds gathered around him, looking at the evil Sisera. Here now lay the lifeless, massive body that had put so much fear into the hearts of all the men and women in Israel.

Some congratulated Barak, but he held up his hands and called with a loud voice, "No! No! Men of Israel, it wasn't I who killed this wicked Sisera. He died at the hands of a Kenite woman named Jael. Deborah's prophesy has come to pass! Jael slew Sisera with just a hammer and a tent nail."

With a loud voice, they all shouted, "Great is the Lord God of Israel and Jael, His deliverer and conqueror! Jael blessed above women!"

Leaving the burial of the giant Sisera and his drowned army to his soldiers, Barak chose several of his best men of war and went full speed after King Jabin. As he entered the king's court, a few of the royal guardsmen came against them but were quickly slain by Barak and his men.

Barak found Jabin in his bedchamber, hiding under a table that held a small incense altar to his god, Baal. Like a child begging and crying, Jabin fell to his knees, pleading for Barak to spare his life.

Jabin held his arms close to his chest, hiding the huge knife he clutched in readiness for an attack. He offered Barak huge sums of money, the choicest concubines, and the best rooms in his palace.

Barak answered, "Those who show mercy shall receive mercy." Jabin looked up at him in surprise and unfolded his arms in preparation to stand. Then Barak added, with a loud voice, "And those who live by the sword shall also die by the sword!"

He saw the glimmer of light on the knife's edge in Jabin's hand as he said "sword" for the first time. The evil king's deceitfulness did not surprise Barak, and he was ready as Jabin drew his arm back to stab upward at him.

With one great swing of his sword, he cut off the head of Jabin, the wicked king. Then Barak made the long journey back to the palm tree where Deborah, the prophetess and judge, awaited him. He gave her his full report of all that had transpired.

As he stood before her, tired and worn, Deborah prophesied by the mouth of God. She told him how God wanted them to write the story about Jael. They were to write songs about her daring work in the slaying of Sisera and put them on a scroll.

Both of them led the army of Israel in worshipping God for several hours. Then they wrote songs and poems about Jael's bravery and sang about her great faith in God.

Barak is listed in the New Testament as one of the heroes of faith (Hebrews 11:32). The land had rest for 40 years after the slaying of Sisera (Judges 5:31).

In all of this, there are great lessons for the wicked who work evil against the people of God, trying to defeat God's divine purpose and plans. Evil should not seek refuge in the house of a woman of God who is blessed above women.

Jael's actions teach us that neither Satan nor evil can triumph against a blessed child of God. We do not always physically kill our enemies. Our anointing from God allows us to kill all evil and wrong-doing with kindness, truth, and love so that our enemies may repent and become born again (see Romans 12:20).

Today, we must pray for all terrorists. Prayer is a greater, more explosive weapon than any man-made bomb. We must know our enemies, confront them, and overcome them with wisdom and the love of God.

Notice how Jael and the Lord Jesus Christ prayed. We must hear and obey the voice of God. With His approval, we may take action for victory. We pray for the unsaved that they might come to know our Lord Jesus Christ and be saved.

Jesus told us, "But I say unto you, which hear, Love your enemies, do good to them which hate you. Bless them that curse you and pray for them who despitefully use you (Luke 6:27-28, see verses 29-38)."

Notice how Sisera came into Jael's tent. If an enemy comes to steal, rape, or kill us, God wants us to become like Jael and hear His voice. Spiritually, our enemies are already dead to God. Only in the name of self-defense should we kill them physically.

Jael was in the right place, position, and season to be used for God's purpose. Sometimes, those in our own households who say they love us the most, may become our worst enemies. "And a man's foes shall be they of his own household (Matthew 10:36)."

Just as Jael killed the evil Sisera and was written about in the holy pages of the Scriptures, we as believers today must kill some things within our own hearts and lifestyles if we are to be counted fit for the Master's use and be blessed above and from above.

Truly being blessed helps us to pass the test of life and overcome trials, troubles, evil thoughts, and imaginations within our own hearts. We must always conclude that the most formidable enemy of all is the one we see in the mirror every day. As we gaze into a mirror, it may be that we still see ourselves and not enough of the Lord Jesus Christ.

Heber Comes Home

Jael stood in the doorway of her tent, watching the horizon long after Barak's chariot departed, carrying the body of Sisera. She was grateful that her neighbors quickly dispersed without asking her questions or intruding. She needed to think.

Her body shook, and her spirit felt even less steady. The enormity of what she had done crashed down on her soul in alternating waves of amazement, shock, glee, nausea, and pride.

"What shall I tell Heber?" She murmured when the black speck of Barak's chariot had finally vanished into the distance. Jael wanted to tell her husband what she had done, to see the pride in his eyes, the amazement, and the wonder. Perhaps now would be a good time to reveal to him her training in weapons and hunting. Perhaps not.

"No, what shall I tell Heber?" She wondered as her legs began to fold with the weakness that washed over her body.

King Jabin was on friendly terms with her husband and his clan— what would her actions do to that peaceful accord? But Heber also did business with the Israelites, so they might have been in danger no matter how the day's battle would have turned out. Perhaps God had also protected her family by leading her to strike down Sisera.

Jael gasped as she remembered the blood and brains that still stained her tent floor. A few hysterical, exhausted giggles escaped her as she stumbled back into her tent and let the door flap fall into place again. She set at work with water, wine, and fuller's earth to clean the thick, coarse matting of the tent's floor.

While the heavy cloth was still damp, she took an awl and thick thread and sewed the hole, then covered the spot with rugs and rearranged the cushions Sisera had shoved out of their usual arrangement. Men, in general, she reflected, were messy creatures. Large men made even larger messes.

Men like Barak, she thought, were sent by God to remove problems.

Jael sat down, hands trembling, her breathing unsteady, as she saw in her memory that adoring, hungry look in Barak's eyes. It disturbed her to realize that another man besides her husband felt love—if that was love and not battlefield emotions—toward her.

"This is wrong. I have done nothing wrong. Yet it is wrong for another man to feel drawn toward me. Lord God Jehovah, did you send this strangeness to humble me after my great victory?" A sigh escaped her half-laughter, half-sob fighting for dominance in her spirit.

The sob won the battle, and Jael curled up on the cushions directly over the spot where she had killed Sisera and wept out her exhaustion and the residue of her fear. Then she slept, and in her dreams, she felt the presence of God again, assuring her that she was His chosen servant, His tool and weapon, who had served Him well and pleased Him greatly.

When Jael woke, she was in darkness because the oil lamps had burned out. She hurried to refill them, wondering why Heber was taking so long to come home. If something evil had happened to him, wouldn't one of his men have run ahead to bring her news? Perhaps silence was the best news of all.

Whatever happened, she decided to welcome him home and make their night together a time of rejoicing and refreshing for their souls. She hurried to wash her face, arrange her hair and change her clothes so she was fresh, clean, and sweet-smelling for him.

She had just stepped back into the main portion of the tent when the door flap was pushed aside, and Heber stood there, staring at her with delight, relief, and awe, making his face glow. The glorious weight of her love for her husband crashed down on Jael.

She ran into Heber's arms, and they kissed as if they had been apart for months. Love came alive; their two hearts became one, passion and desire consuming them both.

Heber tried to talk to Jael, but she covered his words with deep, passionate kisses. Heber looked deep into the eyes of his cherished wife and saw her need for the fulfillment of love.

Effortlessly, he picked her up in his arms and walked towards the bedchamber. He felt her tremble as she placed her strong arms around his neck.

I know my day was strange and wonderful, Heber thought, *but what went on in this tent today?* After the strange events of his long day, he needed to know Jael was safe in his arms again. That was all that mattered, all that had filled his heart and mind as he hurried home.

He knew that now was not the time for words or questions but to allow the dew of passion to guide them into the heights of oneness, to the crest of intimate human endurance.

Hours later, as Jael lay fast asleep, Heber thought about his morning errand that had taken him from their tent so early. When he had left Jael asleep upon their bed, he went to gather the men together to deliver ten new chariots of iron to Jabin, the king, and also to deliver 8,000 shields and swords to the army of Israel.

As far back as he could remember, his people had made metal statues and war items for the surrounding nations. All surrounding nations had great respect for him as a noble of the Kenites and a representative in many matters of trade. No nation had ever dared to war against the Kenite nation before because of their ability to make and supply weapons of warfare.

That morning as he left on his errand, Heber thought, *war is never good.*

Israel's army was so very small, yet their God had kept them through many years of wars. Heber thought about his gods of wood and iron, which he had grown up so tired of. He loved Jael all the more because her distaste for the household gods was clear, yet she never hounded him or did anything to make him miserable enough to abandon the gods of his ancestors.

Her love for the God of Israel was clear, yet she never lectured him about the superiority of Jehovah over his household gods. He knew Jael understood him because where another woman would justify constant nagging as evidence of her love for her husband, she knew that irritating him would only make him determined to hold fast to his gods. Jael lived her beliefs and left him free to decide for himself.

What kind of God was this God of Israel to make a woman so strong and wise?

"Well," he had said out loud, "I'm going to see just what the God of Israel is all about today. If the God of Israel can deliver His people from Sisera and Jabin, He is truly the God of all gods, and most certainly, I will serve Him."

If Israel won the war, he would surprise Jael and ask to meet with her friend, the Levite Joab, to learn about the God of Israel and worship Him in whatever way the Israelites permitted.

Heber always had second thoughts and misgivings when he dealt with Sisera and Jabin, and part of him hoped they would indeed be defeated today. However, a man who understood the mechanics of war knew there was no way they could lose—even against the 8,000 shields and swords he would deliver to Israel today.

Heber never cared for or trusted that evil Sisera, even though he paid Heber well for his weapons. Sisera never complained about Heber's workmanship or the price of the weapons. But his voice and character were so cold, his attitude was ruthless, and his great eyes always looked at people like a lion sizing up its prey.

Heber went first to Hazor to deliver the chariots of iron that Sisera and Jabin had ordered and paid for. Then he went to Israel's camp and delivered many weapons of war to Deborah and Barak. All in all, it was a very profitable day for Heber, and the sun had barely risen on the day of battle.

He had a strange moment when he met with Deborah after delivering the swords and shields to Barak and his sub-commanders. The female judge prophesied to him as if she knew the thoughts going through his head before he arrived at the Israelites' war camp.

As if that were not startling enough, she then gifted him with a small scroll and told him it contained some of the sacred writings of Israel, words given directly from the mouth of Yahweh. Deborah smiled and seemed to hold back laughter when Heber wondered how she knew he could read.

"Your wife has brought you many blessings and gifts, Heber, the royal son of the Kenites. Use one of her gifts to you and finish the journey your mind and heart have begun this day." Then she made a gesture of blessing to him and dismissed him.

Heber took his men far enough from the lines of the battle that they would not be mistaken for enemies by either side, and they had settled down in what shade they could find to await the battle's outcome. Then he opened the scroll and read the history of the Israelites and their interaction with their God, who brought them out of Egypt surrounded by signs and wonders.

Heber had already heard some of these stories because some of his ancestors had been involved in helping the Israelites journey from Egypt for many years. Part of him had been intrigued to learn these were not fantastic tales exaggerated for the benefit of little children's ears but the truth recorded by another nation. Part of him had shuddered at this further proof that the God of Israel, the God his beloved Jael worshipped, was indeed alive and active and moving among His people in the present.

As he now lay beside Jael in their bed, Heber remembered how suddenly a loud shout rang out, saying that Israel had defeated Sisera and his army, and none left alive except Sisera, Jabin, and the four kings who fled for their lives.

When he heard that Barak was chasing Sisera to the territory of Zaanaim, Heber thought of Jael, probably all alone in their tent. A chill of fear had run through his whole being.

Sisera knew where he lived and knew his family was friendly to Jabin. No one else was likely to offer shelter to Sisera after such a monumental defeat in battle.

But knowing what he did about Sisera, Heber knew the giant brute would carelessly disregard the laws of hospitality and take whatever he wanted, including the beautiful woman who was all alone in her tent.

Quickly, Heber mounted his horse and rode towards Zaanaim as fast as he could. Along the way, he passed men who shouted bits and pieces of news of the aftermath of the battle to him. They told him how God had fought for them.

They told him how a miraculous flood had destroyed Sisera's army. They told him that Jabin had died by the sword of Barak. Then, as his tent came within sight, Heber heard about the death of Sisera at the hands of a Kenite woman.

Heber's horse was moving as quickly as it could, but he urged it to go faster, desperate to ensure his precious Jael was safe. His first prayer to the God of Israel was a plea for the well-being of his beloved wife.

He made up his mind that he would serve the true and living God who created all heaven and earth. Although only his horse heard him, he spoke aloud, renouncing the false gods he had served and repented before the Almighty God.

As Heber now lay beside Jael, reliving the momentous day when the region's history and his own life had changed decisively, he felt great peace and joy in his heart that he had never experienced. He was glad of his decision to become a servant of the same God that Jael served.

I have come home at last, Heber thought. Then, to avoid awakening his sleeping wife, he closed his eyes and said a prayer in his heart.

HEBER'S PRAYER

"Dear Jehovah, God of all heaven and earth; the God of Abraham, Isaac, and Jacob, who created all things and knows all things. I thank You for my wife, Jael, for keeping her safe in my absence. I ask You to forgive me for all of my many sins, for the years of serving the false gods of metal, wood, and stone."

"I now confess that You are the only true and living God. I promise to serve You and see Your face as You have shown Yourself to Jael and many others in times past. Help me to know Your ways. Surely I am but a vapor in Your presence. Save me according to Your Word and guide me into new life everlasting."

"Lord God of Israel, please give us sons and daughters. My wife is terribly vexed in that she is still barren. I promise we shall raise our seed to serve You. Amen."

It may have been the cool breeze that suddenly gave Heber the pleasant chill that ran throughout his entire body from head to toe. It could have been just his imagination, the still, small voice he heard that said, "It shall be so."

Heber never fully knew or understood because he fell into a deep, peaceful sleep.

CHAPTER II

REVENGE OF SISERA'S MOTHER

T he mother of Sisera looked out a window and cried through the lattice, "Why is his chariots so long coming? Why tarry the wheels of his chariots (Judges 5:28)?"

Sisera's mother, Adah, was well advanced in years. Her neighbors feared her because of her son's cruelty and because, despite her age, she looked like a young woman.

Everyone knew she had great magic at her command, and it was rumored that she was the lover of sorcerer Zalbazzar. She did nothing to confirm or deny those rumors, and she used the fear of everyone around her to her advantage.

As most mothers did, Adah believed Sisera was just misunderstood because of his giant size, and his enemies were just envious of his high position as commander of the king's army. Although he brutal- ized everyone who crossed him, he treated her with respect and did her bidding.

Adah suspected Sisera did not respect or love her but treated her well because he feared the sorcerer who kept her young and beautiful. That did not matter to her. She lived for her son's every whim.

When neighbors dared to complain about how Sisera treated their daughters, she ignored them as jealousy and blamed the girls for tempting Sisera. When the fathers complained too long or had powerful friends who could make trouble for her beloved son, she sent out her servants who knew how to kill in many subtle or painful ways.

Anyone who tried to deny Sisera whatever he wanted was punished in some small way. If they made too much trouble for her, they were killed, and their children and wives were murdered or kidnapped and sold into slavery.

No one could match her knife skills; she was her son's first teacher in the art of killing. When angry, she was fully capable of slipping through the night to kill her enemies with her bare hands. They all— male and female, old and young alike—died quick, painful deaths.

She was proud of her son and sure that everyone was jealous of him. She was realistic in some matters, including Sisera's love for drinking. Adah had two men who always watched Sisera's every move to ensure that no one took advantage of her son when he was in a drunken stupor.

If anyone offended or threatened him, especially when he could not defend himself, she would command her spies to kill him or her. She was sure they would even kill Jabin, the king, if she paid them enough.

The day of battle had gone on far longer than she had expected. She wondered how the war with Israel was going. Israel was no match for her son! She was so proud of him. He had never lost a battle.

She went down into her underground room, lined with statues of all the gods of Canaan, and sat down to work the magic she had learned from her lover. She filled her silver scrying bowl with black oil and looked into its depths.

The images were confusing, showing water, lightning, and chariots bogged down in the mud. Men wearing the emblem of Hazor lay dead, and she saw no one who looked like the Israelites anywhere among the dead.

Why were Sisera's chariots so long to return from battle? Adah left her room and returned to the upper room of the house, where she could look out through the lattice and see a long way off across the city. There was no sign of anyone returning from the battle.

Her limited patience snapped. She sent for her two evil spies whom she had not sent into battle. They were skilled in killing from the shadows and had no skill in honest warfare on the field of battle.

When they came and bowed before her, she commanded them, "Go! Find my son and bring him back home."

They disappeared into the shadows just as quickly as they had come. Sisera's mother never slept that night.

Early the next morning, the two spies returned, bowed before her, and whispered the news with fear and trembling: Jael, the Kenite woman, had killed Sisera. Barak had taken Sisera's body and buried it with the other thousands of dead soldiers from Sisera's army.

Adah bent over in pain, shrieked in a fury, and fainted at the news of her son's death. The two spies tended to her out of fear of her rage. She awoke to madness, with the strength of a woman twice her size and half her age, going on a rampage of destruction through her house.

The two spies, who had seen so much filth and evil in her service, were frozen in shock. That was their undoing. She saw them, and in her fractured mind, she connected them with her pain and loss.

Quicker than a striking snake, she drew a knife and leaped on them. One died with her knife through his throat. The other fled while his partner died, leaping out the window.

The smell of blood and the stink of death broke through the madness, bringing some sense and fragments of sanity back to her.

"I will kill Jael and Barak!" Adah raged. "They are responsible for my son's death! I shall have my revenge for my son. No one shall stop me!" She vowed.

She armed herself with four knives, their blades dipped in poison, wrapped herself in the ragged black robes of an old woman, and smeared her face with ashes to make herself look aged and poor. Adah heard Sisera speak with contempt of Heber and his wife, how they were soft-hearted fools who gave to the poor and aged. She would take advantage of Jael's soft heart and come close to her in the guise of an infirmed old woman. She would plunge all her daggers into that soft heart and slash that beautiful face and watch Jael suffer and die in agony from the poison that would fill her blood.

THE ATTEMPT ON JAEL'S LIFE

Jael awoke as usual, long before Heber, and said her morning prayers to God. She felt nervous as she waited for Heber to awaken, knowing she had to tell him what happened in their tent before someone else did.

To keep from waking him before he was ready, she went from their bedchamber to the main room of the tent and found the bag Heber had dropped when he came in and swept her up in his arms.

To her surprise, she found a scroll inside. It didn't look like the small hand-sized scrolls Heber used for his tallies when he conducted trade. She trembled a little when she recognized some markings on the outside, but couldn't believe she had read them right. This could not be one of the scripture scrolls of Hebrews.

Whispering a prayer for understanding, she sat down and unrolled the scroll. She found a few blades of grass braided together, marking the place where the reader had stopped. Heber had a bad habit of doing that. She couldn't remember the number of times she had scolded him for treating a scroll that way.

Jael laughed with tears in her eyes as she realized that was proof that Heber had been reading the scroll. It didn't matter how or why he had been reading that scroll; Jael knew God had touched her husband's heart.

Shoving the scroll out of her way so she would not damage it, she pressed her face to the rugs of the tent floor, weeping silently, giving praise and thanks to Jehovah that her husband had taken such an important step toward sharing the faith that was so precious to her.

Her heart was so full of joy that Jael couldn't sit still. She needed to run, if only to use up all the bubbling energy within her so she wouldn't awaken Heber too soon.

She put on the sturdy, enclosed sandals she used when she ran and peeled off her outer robes so her limbs were free to move. Then, with a joyous heart, she went out into the early morning dew and ran like the wind. She felt the anointing of her God upon her life strongly today.

Yet, she felt uneasy and was not sure why. As a young deer full of speed, Jael ran. The only noise that could be heard was the sound of her feet. The early morning creatures of her day beheld her as she flew across the flatlands and climbed the highest hills.

Jael ran for miles. As she came back to the doorway of her tent, she noticed a movement from the corner of her eye. Suddenly, a cloaked figure leaped out of the shadows at her.

She saw the bright glitter of a knife as it arced up toward her throat. Taken completely by surprise, Jael hesitated for just a moment. It almost cost her life. With no time to think, she responded just as she did when Zabed and his evil men attacked her.

With the speed of a lioness, she took hold of the hand that held the knife and twisted her whole body, turning herself and her attacker around. Using the momentum of her enemy, she drove the knife backward into the heart of her attacker.

Adah was utterly surprised at the speed and strength of Jael. She gasped, too stunned to scream as the poisoned knife entered her heart, and fell to the ground, mortally wounded.

Just as stunned, Jael took a few steps back, watching the woman who attacked her for no reason.

"Who are you?" Jael asked, knowing the stranger had but a few seconds to live. "Why did you attack me?"

"I am Sisera's mother," she replied. "That should answer enough for you."

A moan escaped her, and she arched her back as the poison burned as it spread through her blood. Foam appeared on her lips, and her eyes rolled back in her head.

One servant emerged from the tent and saw Jael and the shuddering form on the ground in front of her. He came running, concerned for his master's wife.

Jael signaled him to silence as he stared at the sight of the woman, wracked with spasms of pain, foaming at the mouth. It took only a few more moments for Adah to die.

Jael tried to feel some pity for her, but she could only feel relief and awe at how narrowly she had avoided death. She gave the servant orders to take the woman's body and bury it far from the tent community, telling no one what he had seen or done for the sake and safety of everyone in Heber's household. Shaken, the young man obeyed.

Shaken and confused, Jael entered her tent. What she saw made her forget what had just happened.

There, where she had left the scroll just a short time before, Heber kneeled in prayer, holding the scroll reverently in his outstretched hands, just as she had seen Joab the Levite do.

Feeling a nudge in her spirit, Jael stepped outside and looked around the clear area before their tent. All the spots where the household idols had stood were now empty. Even the small platforms and stone pillars they stood on were gone.

With tears of gratitude and thanksgiving flowing down her cheeks, Jael entered the tent and thanked God, who answers all prayers. She kneeled beside her husband, and they worshipped God together for the first time.

That day, Jael and Heber talked. She gladly shared with Heber all the events of her life she had never told him before. She disclosed everything, including the death of her parents and her Aunt Modessa at the hands of Zabed, the Terrible; the attempted revenge of Zaltura, the thief; Sisera's death in their tent; and the attack by Sisera's mother.

Heber shared with Jael his new faith in the true and living God of Israel. Kneeling before Jael, Heber tenderly took her hand, looked into her eyes, and promised to love and protect her forever and to serve God as long as he lived.

With passion and joy, they embraced; their two hearts became one, and the presence of God filled the tent. Heber knew Jael, his precious diamond, was truly blessed above women. Like Abraham and Moses, he was blessed above men to have her as his wife, a woman blessed above by God.

CHAPTER 12
JAEL MEETS PROPHETESS DEBORAH

J ael was troubled as she sat on the edge of the bed, combing her long dark hair. She had just returned from a long visit meeting with her aunt's scholarly friends.

The freedom and equality between male and female, between the different nations and races that these thoughtful, educated people shared, contrasted sharply with what she had seen the last time she went to the marketplace in Hazor with her servants. There, she had seen slaves on the auction block and later overheard one man convince another to sell his daughter into a brothel.

In the marketplace, a woman who walked alone was accosted by men who assumed she was a harlot. She was in danger of being taken against her will unless a man came running to her rescue and claimed a blood tie or some relationship that gave him authority over her. A shopkeeper insulted another woman, and her husband raised a furious ruckus until the shopkeeper apologized. The same shopkeeper insulted another woman, and her husband laughed.

A man could push a woman down and steal from her with no recourse unless her father, brother, son, or husband were there to protest and demand justice. Unless a woman had a vicious tongue and knew how to defend herself with a knife or stick, she rarely had any recourse on her own.

Men were always presumed to be stronger and in the right. The only women who walked in safety and with honor and respect were the priestesses and temple prostitutes, but Jael would not wish such a life on anyone, no matter how much prestige it offered.

She had grown up knowing that was how the world worked, but Jael's spirit was heavy that day. Perhaps the contrast between her Canaanite heritage and the safety and respect afforded most of the women in Israel seemed stronger than ever.

Jael had shared with their group a long list of laws that protected Hebrew women. Widows had a right to ask for protection, and girls who were betrayed, seduced, or raped had some small claim to justice against their oppressors. They were small laws, and Joab admitted that they did little good unless a woman knew the laws and could find a scribe or priest who would support her claim.

Still, Jael wished the kingdoms of Canaan would adopt such laws. The women of Israel did not enjoy the equality and freedom her scholarly friends did, but it was a step in what Jael considered the right direction.

It had taken many years for Jael to sense and then put into words what she now believed: that there was no difference between male and female souls when they stood before Jehovah God. The problem was that so few in Canaan worshiped the One True God, and she doubted she could ever obtain an audience with the High Priest in the Hebrews' Tabernacle to present her beliefs before him.

Jael knew the first step to ensure the freedom and safety of women everywhere, without requiring them to have a male protector, was to bring the entire world to know, worship, and acknowledge the One True God. That endeavor might take thousands of years if it was ever accomplished.

Jael wanted something done immediately. This dilemma of male arrogance had to be resolved. While many had called her blessed above women, she knew that women were not treated fairly in the decision-making policies of the city, the government, or their religion.

"I must do something," Jael said out loud. "And do something I most certainly will!"

She had heard that Deborah, the judge, had experienced many problems and controversies as a female leader over Israel. Jael wondered how she could meet Deborah to discuss this serious issue.

"Why, Barak, of course!" she exclaimed. She knew Barak was very close to Deborah, and she heard some of the songs they had written about her. Jael went to see Barak.

Barak was sitting under one of Deborah's palm trees when he noticed Jael coming toward him. There was the woman he loved in his heart, but the law and his devotion to God forbade him to express his feelings openly. Slowly he walked towards her, never taking his eyes off hers. His heart beat faster, and his knees wobbled.

With dignity and honor, Jael smiled at him and asked, "May I speak to you?"

"But of course," Barak said, ashamed of himself for being so slow to speak. "How may I serve you, oh great woman of God?"

Jael spent the next hour sharing with Barak her deep concern about the plight of the women in her country. She revealed that she knew of the laws of the Israelites that granted women some protection, and her hope was that, somehow, the Israelite leaders could influence at least their Canaanite allies to grant the same protection and dignity to the women of their cities.

"It isn't nearly enough, but it is a start. The first step in a long journey," Jael added. "Someday, men and women will stand openly as equals before God and all peoples."

"Equals?" Barak nearly laughed aloud, but he saw Jael's earnestness. Where had she come up with such ideas? He questioned her cautiously, trying not to commit himself to supporting her outlandish, immodest ideas.

It didn't take long for Jael to reveal the group of strange, scholarly folks of many religious beliefs and races, men and women, sitting as equals at a common table. The mental image this generated fascinated and repelled him at the same time.

He had evidence that women were indeed as courageous, strong, and intelligent as men, but those were special exceptions, such as Jael and Deborah. He shuddered at the thought of women everywhere going into battle alongside men, working as blacksmiths, traveling as merchants, and filling other occupations that were dangerous and better left to men.

Jael seemed to be encouraged by his silence and startled him with the suggestion that a good first step in bringing change to both Jews and Canaanites was to ask Deborah to send a letter of protest to the council of elders in Hazor and the local Hebrew leaders and ask them to come together for the good of all women.

Barak tried to discourage Jael, but it was not to be.

Jael simply smiled and said softly, "Lead me to Deborah, please."

Barak imagined she had that same determined look in her eyes when she lifted the hammer to kill Sisera. Sighing, he knew it was useless to protest. Better to let Deborah speak some sense to her.

As he rose to take Jael by the hand to help her stand, Deborah appeared from among the palm trees to join them. For a long moment, the two strong women looked at each other, Kenite warrior and Hebrew prophetess. Jael stood up without Barak's help.

Deborah smiled, opened her arms wide, and the two women hugged as if they were long-lost sisters. Barak took a step backward, shivering as a sense of power radiated from them. He had been present several times as the Spirit of Yahweh fell on Deborah, and she prophesied. Barak knew it was about to happen here and now.

The anointing of God fell upon both women. They went to their knees, clasping hands, tears streaming down their faces that glowed with God's power. They prophesied, sang, and testified in unison of the goodness of God.

God told Jael that He was with her and none would be able to stand against her. He told Deborah that she was chosen out of due season with a divine appointment to be the judge and leader of Israel and that her name would stand forever as a guiding light for both women and men.

When the anointing of the Spirit faded away, there was a long silence. Barak offered his hands to the two women, helping them stand, and led them into Deborah's tent so they could have some shelter and privacy as they digested all that the Spirit had revealed to them. He was not surprised when Deborah listened to Jael's idea and agreed to write the letters she requested. Perhaps this was the leading of God. Only time would tell.

CHAPTER 13
THE NEW MOON GAMES

Early one morning, almost a moon after Jael's encounter with Deborah, the council of elders in Hazor made a proclamation.

Scribes wrote many copies of the document and sent it throughout the city and surrounding countryside. It simply stated that if there could be found a woman who could challenge and defeat their best man, Zophar, in the upcoming New Moon Games, they would establish the laws of protection for women proposed by prophetess Deborah of Israel.

The news spread like wildfire throughout the region. All knew that the mighty Zophar had yet to be beaten in any challenge, either in or outside of the New Moon Games. He always defeated the great men who came from many countries near and far. Men of great power, such as Suram the Giant, who had the strength of a lion and legs as swift as a horse. There was also Basor, who ran on both hands and feet with incredible speed, yet Zophar had easily beaten them both.

"Why must it be you?" Heber asked Jael when she told him about her intention to compete in the New Moon Games. "Let one of the other women compete against Zophar."

"Have faith in me, my dear husband, as I have faith in God," was her only reply.

Then came the day of the New Moon Games, which lasted seven days from morning until night. Men were pitted against men in various displays of skill, power, and endurance.

However, this celebration of the New Moon Games was the first in its history to include a woman. Because of this, the arena was filled to capacity and overflowing with people from many nations.

Jael won contest after contest. Men of valor came from far and wide to witness her greatness in the many contests of skill, endurance, speed, and strength. Jael won every contest she entered, and the wagering for and against her grew more frantic as each challenge was met and won.

It was on the seventh day, the last day of the New Moon celebration, that Jael stepped into the arena. As the contests progressed, losers were eliminated, leaving only two contestants: the mighty Zophar and Jael, the Kenite woman. Each was given one choice of a contest in which to challenge the other.

Zophar chose the foot race once around the perimeter of the arena. He was unbeaten in this event, his specialty. When the wagers were placed, Jael received only a fraction of the wages in her favor, despite her many wins up until this point.

"Who could ever beat Zophar the Great? Certainly not a woman," the master of ceremonies shouted.

There was a great roar of laughter and agreement from the crowd. Deborah, who had been present through every event, encouraged Jael. Heber hugged her tight and prayed.

Strutting with full confidence, Zophar went to the starting line of the race and struck a heroic pose. Arrogantly, he threw up his arms, exciting the people. Silently as a cheetah, Jael took her place beside the aggressive, unwise Zophar, who mocked her by sticking out his tongue at her.

All the men shouted. "Zophar, Zophar, the champion of the gods!"

Zophar was truly awesome to behold. All men longed to possess his physique of pure muscle, long limbs, and handsome features.

ZOPHAR MEETS HIS MATCH

Zophar was very proud of his accomplishment over many other great men of his time. *My gods, Baal-Berith and Ashtoreth, have served me quite well*, he thought as he prepared to run against *this foolish woman.*

"Jael," Zophar said, looking down upon her.

"You shall be the first and the last woman ever allowed to participate in the New Moon Games!" He spat on her.

He had heard some of the songs the Hebrews sang about her, and he didn't like any of them, especially the one about how Jael had killed Sisera with just a hammer and a nail. He hadn't cared for the brutal Sisera, but he detested the fact that a woman killed him.

Zophar was a brute to the bone. He had no respect for women and felt their purpose in life was to please and serve men. They were only good for sexual pleasure, cooking, cleaning, and caring for the children.

However, he had watched this woman in the swimming contest. She swam as if she was propelled by some unseen power. She swam like a great fish that actually lived in the waters. She had won every contest she entered. But then again, she had yet to come up against him in any contest until then.

"Well, she won't beat me," Zophar vowed. "Everybody knows that I am the very best! I am the fastest man alive!"

He said out loud as if to encourage and convince himself. Despite towering over her, for some unknown reason, Zophar had a strange feeling that Jael was looking down upon him. Something just didn't feel right. Though it was hot, he felt a chill over his body.

"Who are your gods?" He asked Jael in a rough voice. "Where do they live and rule?"

With a candid smile, Jael looked upon her formidable opponent with the eyes of a lioness and spoke to Zophar with the sweet voice of a nightingale, the same anointed voice with which she had spoken to Sisera.

"Why sir, you don't know the God whom I serve? He is Lord of all. There is no other God like Him. He lives in the heavens above. He fills and rules over the whole universe. His name is Jehovah, the God of the Hebrews, Lord of Lords, and King of Kings. He created all things in Heaven and Earth. He knows all things. He is the one and only God! You ought to consider serving Him today."

"Lies! Foolishness!" Zophar shouted and cursed Jael in the name of his gods.

With mockery, malice, and dishonor, he danced around the arena like an exotic dancer, gyrating his body in the movements women used in the fertility dances all through the New Moon Games. Even a man half-drowned with wine could tell that he mocked Jael, inferring he could take on a woman's role just as she dared to step into the arena reserved for men.

Men and women laughed, shouted, and leaped to their feet with glee, chanting again, "Zophar the Great! Great are the gods of the mighty Zophar! We love you, Zophar!"

Jael stood at the starting line and viewed the course she was about to run. She glanced up at the sky and saw a great face in the clouds.

"My God is here!" She exclaimed. "He is watching over me and I know that He is with me!"

Zophar looked up but saw no one.

As she braced for the signal to start, Jael felt God's presence and His anointing upon her. Deep in her heart, she wished that her parents and Aunt Modessa were there to witness this great race to win something more valuable than any personal acclaim or temporary prize.

Most of the people were for Zophar. God was for Jael. From heaven above, the angels looked down and said, "Run, Jael! God is with you, which is better than ten thousand against you!"

Jael the Conqueror and Zophar the Champion stood on their mark. Side-by-side stood good and evil.

Jael's obstacle became her opportunity. Unlike most of us, she focused on victory in the midst of the problem. She saw success only and never considered defeat. This is true faith.

Like David when he faced Goliath, Jael's heart's desire to win overruled what she saw with her eyes. When we are faced with overwhelming obstacles, we must focus on the answer and not just on the problem. We must set our faith, words, and heart upon the desired results. Jael saw her opposition as a prime opportunity to show the world her glorious God. She ran for the benefit of others, not just for herself.

The signal flag fell, and Jael ran for her life. She knew she represented every woman, young and old, especially those yet to be born.

Immediately, Zophar dashed ahead of Jael.

"Oh, no!" was the cry of the women in the city.

"Hurray!" shouted the men with a roar.

Jael viewed Zophar as the one barrier blocking a change for the betterment of the women of her time. She called on the name of the Lord.

Zophar knew he was far ahead of Jael. As he made the turn at the halfway point, to his surprise, Jael was right behind him. Soon she ran right beside him.

She isn't human! He thought with shock.

Zophar raced to the finish line with all his power, speed, and might. He called upon his gods and used every muscle in his strong frame to get more speed. Jael, stride for stride, passed him by with visible grace and seeming ease.

Jael lifted her hands and cried out in thanks and praises to God as she crossed the finish line five strides ahead of Zophar. Hundreds of women ran out onto the course and smothered her with praises, kisses, hugs, and thanksgiving.

Heber was shocked yet delighted by the skill and speed with which Jael ran. From that day forward, men sang a new song about Jael, how the mighty Zophar bowed down and fell before her, confessing that Jael was truly blessed above women.

POEMS

JAEL, COME AWAY WITH ME

"Jael! Jael!" The wind seemed to whisper.

"Hear my voice, and please listen to me!

I'll take you high up on the mountain tops, and we will tread upon the raging seas."

"We will dash upon the treetops,

Forever there, you will be free.

We will kiss the dew of the sky blue yonder.

Come, Jael, won't you fly away with me?"

"Oh no! Not so!

Cried the rising sun as it crests the early morning dew.

Don't listen to the restless wind, Jael.

Her words are just fooling you!"

"Just follow me; I'll brighten your day.

For in every sunrise, I'll give you light.

Is there anything in the earth more beautiful than my sunset and its glow before the dark of night?"

"Be still, Jael, and hear me!" A bald eagle cried as it spread its great wings high in the morning sky.

"You've seen the ending sunset and felt the restless wind.

Are they more beautiful and trustworthy than I am?"

"Behold! I look high, and I see low.

I build my nest in the highest tree.

I've watched you run pathways each day for miles.

Come quickly, Jael. Come fly away with me!"

The moon spoke enticingly to her in the starlit brightness of the night.

The sea uttered its voice so tenderly, saying,

"Come, Jael, cross over me tonight."

The night owls did hoot from deep within their breasts, Saying, "Follow us, Jael.

We are wise;

We know what you need best."

"I have listened to all of you," Jael replied.

"You are all so precious, so lovely, and so kind,

but I will follow God, who created you all.

I'll fly away with Him. I am His, and He is mine!"

"I hear His voice, and I love Him so. He alone is God.

He's Lord of all;

None of you could deliver me

If I should stumble or fall."

"Can you redeem my soul from sin?

Be my strength, my joy when there's no peace?

Can you ease my pain on my darkest day or

Give eternal life that will never cease?"

"There's none like my God in all the earth.

He's my victory, my joy, and praise.

He has been there when I needed him most

When death stood before me to end my days."

"He is higher than the highest mountain,

Far deeper than the deep blue sea.

He is taking me to my destiny's shores

Where my reward awaits me."

SONG: THE GOD OF ISRAEL

A song Jael sang unto the Lord the morning just before Sisera came running to her tent:

The mountains tremble at your presence;

All of my heart, only you can fill.

The clouds are just as dust on your feet;

You are the God of Israel.

Lord, you are the love of my heart;

I live just to do your will.

The heavens cannot contain all of you;

You are the God of Israel.

You are the Lord God of Israel,

All that you do, no one can tell.

Mending broken wings of every white dove,

And you know that my name is Jael.

I long to see you face to face.

I know you love me still.

My strength, my hope, my life, and my joy,

You are the God of Israel.

I long to be where you are always,

All mine enemies you allowed me to kill.

At the throne of your grace, I'll forever bow;

You are the God of Israel.

Awake! Awake God of Israel.

Arise, let me see your face,

Reveal your presence to my innermost being.

I will praise you in every place.

I'll lift up my voice in that most holy place.

Let all heaven and earth be still.

You are my God; I just can't love you more.

You are the God of Israel.

Of Israel, you are the God of Israel,

Who cancels the plans of kings.

The God of Israel: Oh Israel, oh Israel,

Bows down and worships Him still.

He is worthy of all the praise and glory;

He is the God of Israel, the God of Israel.

Use me, Lord, on the earth.

I rejoice in thee, the God of Israel. He is the God of all Israel.

By: D. R. Downing

CHAPTER 14

IKKESH, THE SON OF SISERA

Ikkesh was an evil man, and he loved it. Just like his father, Sisera, the Giant, he loved the wicked and sinful side of life, such as lying, raping young women, thievery, and killing any man weaker than himself.

Ikkesh (whose name means crooked, perverse, or deceitful) lived up to his name in every way. His mother was a slave who tried to run away many times, both before and after she gave birth to Ikkesh. She vanished the day after Ikkesh killed his first man in a street brawl.

Some hoped she escaped, but others who were more realistic believed that Sisera or even Ikkesh killed her in the drunken celebration that followed his first kill. No one ever knew her name, and it was likely that neither Sisera nor Ikkesh knew or cared what her name was.

While he was not a giant of a man like Sisera, his father, Ikkesh believed he was faster with a knife and sword than his father or any man alive. He stood taller than most men.

Even though it was said he had killed over 50 men by the time he had a full beard, he never had the desire to test his skill against his father in hand-to-hand combat because his father was the captain of Jabin's army. And the fact that a Kenite woman named Jael had killed his father while he lay asleep in her tent was certainly not acceptable to his manhood.

Even though he hated Sisera (as all men did), at the first opportunity, Ikkesh vowed to kill Jael, bring honor to his family name, and more fame in the land for himself. Within his evil mind and wicked heart, he began to plan.

Because Jael was loved by many, and her husband Heber commanded a large company of men, the killing of Jael had to be done in secret. Ikkesh was among the multitude of people during the New Moon Games that observed the race between Jael and Zophar. Unlike the rest of the crowd, he was not surprised that Jael won.

Though he felt in his heart that he could outrun both of them, he knew Jael was a very dangerous and worthy opponent. After all, she had done what no other man except himself could have done: killed his father, Sisera the Giant, and Adah, his evil mother. It was time for Jael to die.

Ikkesh learned Jael often went swimming in the local river by herself. That pleased him because he was an excellent swimmer. He made plans to go to the river the next morning and wait for Jael.

He would hide among the bushes along the edge of the water, leap out at her as she came to the water, kill her, and let the river become her tomb. His plan was perfect.

He smiled at the plan and said to himself, *Ikkesh, you are so very smart; you are so very good!* He spent most of the night eating, drinking, and enjoying his evil plan.

The Kenite tribes had come to a serious point in their history. Their king had died with no heirs and no close male relatives with a clear, strong claim to the leadership.

By this time in their history, they had grown numerous and strong, so they had even built a city which they named Ziaam. Heber had moved his household closer to the walls of Ziaam because, as a member of the ruling family of the Kenites, he had a responsibility to help find a solution to the problem.

As the days of talking and deliberating turned into fortnights, then a month, then two, several claimants to the crown emerged. One of them was Heber.

On the morning of the day Ikkesh planned to kill her, Jael awoke in her tent before dawn, thinking about the possibility of Heber being named king. It could be any day now.

While being queen did not excite Jael, she knew Heber was the best man for the job. She was too restless with anticipation, wondering if this was the day Heber would return from meeting with the Kenite leadership with the news that he had been named king.

To avoid waking Heber, Jael slipped out of bed, dressed, and left the tent. She decided to take a long swim, and if that did not help steady her and work off her restless anticipation, she would run before returning in time to make breakfast for Heber and pray with him before he went into the city.

As the darkness of the night faded into the dawning of a new day, Jael noticed that all was quiet. Too quiet, she thought as she headed for the river. No morning songbirds were singing, nor were the many voices of the mating creatures of the forest present.

She prayed silently, asking God's blessing on Heber and their future as she approached the riverbank. Her distraction almost caused Jael to lose her precious life.

As she stepped down into the water, Ikkesh leaped out from his hiding place in the bushes with a knife pointed at her throat. Jael had no time to draw her knife and defend herself against his attack. Her long-ago training with Aunt Modessa leaped into her mind.

Lunging out into deep water, in one quick, fluid motion, faster than the eye could see, she took a deep breath and did a backward flip that took her out of harm's way to the bottom of the river. Then she swam as fast as she could to cross to the other side of the river. She sensed her attacker was not far behind her, but she knew better than to look back.

As Jael reached the other side of the river and ascended its banks, she looked behind her. The man who had attacked her was only a few lengths away. She could see his huge frame and demonic eyes glaring at her.

Jael wasn't in the mood to kill or be killed. She ran through the forest faster than ever before, yet her enemy was not far behind her. In fact, he had drawn closer to her.

He is faster than Zophar! Jael refused to let that thought discourage her.

Knowing she could not outrun him, her only defense was in the trees. Jael looked for a suitable tree where she could defend herself. She could hear her enemy's footsteps drawing closer and closer.

Pushing hard, Jael leaped, grabbed a low-hanging branch, swung herself up, and ran up the nearest tree as her aunt had taught her so long ago.

Ikkesh had not planned for things to go like this. From the moment he had leaped out of the bushes at Jael, the shock of his size and presence should have stunned her, giving him just the time he needed to cut off her head and feed her to the creatures of the river.

His knife that had never missed before missed Jael when she did a backward dive he had never seen. As he chased her underwater, his respect for her grew, especially seeing her climb the riverbank and run through the forest like a deer in flight, as if she hadn't already swum the width of the river.

With all of his might and speed, he ran after Jael. Just as his father had run to Jael's tent to his death, Ikkesh ran to the tree Jael now climbed. With all of his strength, he clambered up after her.

Jael shouted down at Ikkesh, "Why are you trying to kill me? I have done you no harm!"

When Ikkesh responded, his deep raspy voice reminded her of the voice of Sisera, the Giant.

"I am Ikkesh, the son of Sisera, whom you killed in your tent, and I have come to rape and kill you. I shall cut off your head, hands, feet, and ears and feed your eyes to the birds and your tongue to the wolves," he shouted and never paused in his climbing.

Again, Jael had no choice. She transformed herself from Jael, the wife of Heber, into Jael the Conqueror. As a great lioness preparing to kill or a great female ape defending her territory, Jael let out a victory cry that sent chills down the spine of Ikkesh and made his blood turn to ice.

She unsheathed the long dagger that her Aunt Modessa had given her years ago. In one quick motion, Jael caught a vine, leaped down onto the back of Ikkesh, and drove her dagger deep into his body.

Ikkesh screamed: the sound of his voice choked off with a gush of blood as Jael's knife pierced his ribs, slicing through his lung, aided by the force of all her weight slamming into him.

As they both fell to the ground, Jael used the body of Ikkesh to cushion her fall. Ikkesh died, his body broken by the impact, and Jael was knocked unconscious by the force of the fall.

How long she lay unconscious, Jael did not know, nor what brought her back to reality. Even though it was full morning and the sun was shining, there was darkness all around her, with daylight a short distance away.

There were no sounds of nature, only a putrid stench and stillness like death. The smell was so odorous that Jael could hardly breathe.

She leaped to her feet and looked into the dense foliage around her. What she saw made her skin crawl and her blood turn to ice. While Jael feared rats and snakes, what she saw was greater by far than what she could imagine.

Right in front of her was a snake, nearly 20 cubits in length, with huge lifeless, slanted eyes, the size of large buzzard eggs, void of all emotion, observing her as a tasty meal. When Jael tried to run and retrieve her dagger from the body of Ikkesh, she found she could not move her body. She was completely under the power of this giant snake.

Jael remembered when she was just a little girl in her bed, and when she had turned back the covers, a huge snake was lying there. She had screamed as loud as she could for as long as she could, even after her father had killed it.

Jael was brought back to reality when the giant snake moved closer to her. The stench increased, and the warm morning air around her became colder than a winter's blast. The snake had the head of a man.

There appeared to be hundreds of creatures of all shapes and sizes, like various animals, giant bugs, and winged insects all around him. Somehow, Jael knew they were the demonic spirits she had learned about from Joab the Levite. What happened next would make a thousand brave warriors faint or flee for their lives.

The giant serpent opened its mouth and spoke to Jael, saying: "I am Satan, the prince of darkness, the god of this world, the god of Sisera, Ikkesh, and Zabed the Terrible, my servants whom you have killed. Jael, if you will bow down to worship me, you shall live. If you refuse to serve me, you will surely die."

Then Satan made his move. Right before Jael's eyes, Satan transformed himself into an angel of light, the most beautiful angelic being with a wingspan of over 16 cubits. A desire to touch him came over Jael, but due to the stench of his unwashed body, a reflection of the filth of his rebellious spirit appeared, and she was able to overcome her desire.

Seeing that his angelic form didn't move Jael to worship, Satan tried the next best thing: to deceive and seduce her. He transformed himself into a man; the most well-built, handsome, and desirable human being Jael had ever seen (see 2 Corinthians 11:13-15).

This is pure witchcraft and sorcery of the highest form, she thought. Immediately, she realized that standing before her was the father and creator of all black magic.

Jael's heart skipped a beat as her whole body was filled with temptation and lust far greater than any desire she had ever known, even for her husband. As Satan reached out his evil hands to touch Jael, to mate with her and consume her, Jael felt her spirit rise up and come alive within her.

With boldness, firmness, and words flowing from the depths of her heart and soul, Jael spoke directly into the face of Satan. Knowing she had no power over him and that there was no knife or sword on earth that could be used against him, she chose the only weapon to use she knew: her love for God and her moral standards as a woman of God.

"Satan," she said, "you are not a true and living god at all. I have read about you, that you are nothing but a liar and a thief, the god of sin, sickness, death, and disease."

"My God, Jehovah Elohim, whom I love and serve, is an everlasting God, the creator of Heaven and Earth, the God of love, joy, and peace, and He gives life everlasting. I will never leave Him, for He is the only true and living God of all Heaven and Earth. He alone is Lord of Lords and Kings of Kings."

"Until I die, I will trust Him, worship Him, and call upon His great name. I refuse to bow down or serve you. You are a fake, false imitation of God, and besides all this, you stink."

Satan's countenance immediately changed into his true form of demonic proportions, standing over seven cubits tall with a tail that seemed to stretch further into the forest than Jael could see. With a voice that sent chills down Jael's spine, Satan said, "Now you will die, Jael. I shall eat you and consume you as wheat."

Satan stretched forth his hands to kill and destroy Jael. Suddenly, the area behind her became brighter than the noonday sun.

Once again, the Angel of the Lord stood beside Jael and spoke directly to Satan with a voice of like many rivers of living waters, saying, "Remove yourself from this place, Satan, and do not touch my servant, Jael. She is a chosen vessel to do my will and obey my commands."

Immediately, like a great puff of smoke exploding into the air, Satan disappeared. Then the Angel of the Lord turned towards Jael, and as Jael looked into his eyes full of love and compassion, she knew he was the same one she had met before, who came to her and gave her strength and comfort in the home of her Aunt Modessa.

Jael wanted to hold him, touch him, and express her undying love for him, but she still couldn't move her body. He opened his mouth again and said: "Fear not, Jael, for I am with you always, just as I have told you before. You shall go forth in the Earth and fight many battles, but I will be with you and with your children forever."

Then he reached out a finger and touched her shoulder. Jael fell down and lay prostrate before the Lord in worship, giving honor, glory, and thanksgiving with all of her might.

Time stood still. Nothing else mattered more to Jael than being in God's divine presence.

Jael felt someone gently shaking her shoulders. She opened her eyes and saw a strange man bent over her.

Faster than lightning strikes, Jael rolled over on the ground, caught the man by his throat with both hands and placed both feet upon his abdomen, lifting him into the air, throwing him a far distance. As a leopard attacks her prey, Jael quickly draws her dagger out of the body of Ikkesh and runs to where the stranger lies stunned.

She was ready to kill him to defend herself. Surely he had to be a friend of Ikkesh.

Before she could kneel on his chest and place the knife to his throat, he screamed, "Jael, Jael; I am Bezer! Don't you remember me? Please don't kill me! I mean you no harm!"

Jael's mind went back to her childhood and remembered how God had used her to change the life of Bezer, the Bully.

After defeating Bezer in a fight, she made him promise to change, and he did so. It had been years since she had heard anything about him, and she had left her home village when she married Heber. Her relief at seeing a semi-familiar face and knowing he was an old friend made her overlook the slight twinge of warning, the hint of something dark in his eyes.

Jael grabbed Bezer by the hand, and after pulling him to his feet, she hugged him, saying, "Oh, I am so sorry, Bezer! Please forgive me!"

They sat down on a large rock to laugh and talk about the past. Bezer shared with Jael his experiences as a warrior in various armies and men he met who sang songs about her, written by Barak and prophetess Deborah, how Jael had become a conqueror and deliverer of women bound by men.

Jael looked deep into his eyes and said, "Why are you here, Bezer? Tell me what you want."

Bezer said, "I am a hired mercenary, paid to capture or kill Ikkesh, the son of Sisera. I see you already did my job for me. Again, I am indebted to you. I saw him attack you at the river, but I cannot swim. Do you remember when we fought on that bridge, where I was throwing rocks into the river?"

"Why yes, I remember," said Jael.

"Well, it wasn't just to try to hit the fish. I was also afraid of the river. Today, I had to run back to get my horse when I saw Ikkesh attack you. I rode him across the river and came as quickly as I could to help you and capture Ikkesh. But you must go quickly now, Jael, because I have heard of a plot to capture and kill your husband to keep him from becoming king in Ziaam."

Jael's heart seemed to stop beating, and great fear gripped her soul. Heber to be killed? Quickly, she stood up and ran home to warn

Heber of this impending danger. She would fight for him and kill anyone if necessary. Jael loved Heber more than life itself.

As Bezer watched Jael run across the land faster than a young deer or mountain goat, his countenance changed to the evil villain he was. He laughed out loud as he remembered the look on Jael's face as she believed all the lies that he had told her.

Well, he said to himself, *what I told her about Ikkesh was true, but all those lies about being afraid of the water are pure hogwash. I can swim better than Jael, or anyone else, for that matter.*

As he lifted the dead Ikkesh upon the back of his horse, he thought about his assignment, which was to capture or kill Heber, Jael's husband. Heber wanted to become the king of Ziaam. In secret, Bezer worked for Zalbazzar, the sorcerer, who had promised he would be king if he killed or captured Jael's husband.

"I shall be king!" Bezer said to himself. He knew Heber was to meet with the council of elders later that morning, which was the perfect opportunity to capture his next quarry.

"This place sure does stink," he said as he climbed up into the saddle, and the smell of decay, rottenness, and putrefaction filled his nostrils. Bezer the Bully would have run for his life if he had looked closely into the underbrush and seen the huge snake with the head of a man that followed him, listening to his every word, making plans, and plotting his next move, which is always to kill, steal, and destroy.

As Jael approached her tent, her exhaustion from her busy morning caught up with her. How could she have encountered Ikkesh, Satan, and Bezer in such a short period of time?

The sun was barely above the horizon. She wanted to go back to bed and sleep the day away, yet there was joy in her heart as she remembered encountering the Angel of the Lord. Oh, how she loved the Lord Jehovah, the true and living God!

She gave a sigh of relief when she saw everything was normal, and Heber sat in his favorite chair in front of their tent. Jael ran to him with tears of joy and love filling her eyes. Embracing him, she shared her concerns and all that Bezer had told her about the plan to kill him and stop him from becoming king.

Heber laughed as he lifted his precious jewel into his arms, kissing her and reassuring her that everything would be alright. Oh, how he loved that woman. As he carried Jael into the tent and then into their bedchamber, he could sense there was much more to Jael's morning experience than she had told him.

Heber thought, *I still have a few moments to spend with my lovely wife before I meet with the elders about becoming king. There is no better way for me to begin my day than to be intimate with my wife.*

As Jael's great kisses upon Heber's body and lips infused passion and his words of desire into her ears spoke of his desire for mating in the morning, with great need and expectation, they came together as one body, one heart, mind, and soul. Lovemaking took them across hills that no mortal couple could climb, and passion took them across living waters far too deep to measure.

Both were propelled into a higher plane of utopia and bliss greater than either had ever experienced before. Soon, both fell into a deep sleep of satisfied passion that provided much-needed peace and rest.

When Jael awoke, she saw Heber had already left for his meeting. She prayed for him, asking Jehovah, her God, to guide and keep him safe.

As Jael thought about all the changes in her life, she was over-whelmed with the pain of missing her parents and her Aunt

Modessa. Her thoughts brought tears to her eyes. Jael realized she had not returned to her birthplace in over two years.

"Well," she said to herself, "I will not delay any longer. I shall go there today and pay my respects to them." After taking care of her morning chores and giving the servants work for the rest of the day, she left a message for Heber. With much anticipation, Jael rode towards her old home.

Meanwhile, Heber, as he rode toward Ziaam, was very happy at the thought of becoming king and having Jael as queen at his side.

"Why, heaven cannot be any better than this!" He said, remembering the intimate passion of the morning lovemaking. He was so engrossed in the pleasure of his thoughts that he didn't hear the whistle of the rock shot from a slingshot, streaking through the air, aiming straight for his head. There was pain, then darkness, and then there was nothing, nothing at all.

Bezer cautiously approached Heber, lying prostrate and unconscious on the ground. He was very pleased with his day's accomplishments and tomorrow's prospects. He ignored the horse that ran away when Heber fell from the saddle. As he looked down upon Heber, he was surprised to find he was not dead, but seriously wounded.

"Well," he said, as he lifted Heber and slung him across the back of his horse, "my job is to bring them in dead or alive, and I have one dead and one yet alive."

NIGHTWIND

As Jael arrived at her childhood home, she remembered her early childhood days and teenage years. As she got off her horse, she looked around and noticed that not much about the village had changed.

Everyone was busy with their afternoon work or preparing for the evening meal, and there was no one to greet or question her as she walked to the outskirts of the village and the grove surrounded by Canaanite idols, where her parents were buried. As she stood at the graves of Zamu and Hadassah, she couldn't help but cry many tears, especially when she remembered the times of her disobedience, defiance, and the pain she caused them.

Just as she was about to leave to go to the gravesite of her Aunt Modessa, Jael heard the scream of a horse in full fury. Turning, she saw a black shadow emerge from the hills and race toward her horse. Jael stood still, knowing there was nothing more dangerous than putting herself between two horses locked in battle.

Her horse, a young stallion newly broken to the saddle, reared and screamed in return and then bolted, fleeing the advances of the enormous black horse. Jael could only guess that the other horse was a wild stallion, protecting his territory and his herd, hidden somewhere in the hills beyond her former village. She wished she had ridden a gelding today, but it was too late to rethink that decision.

The sun was descending to evening, and if she had to make the entire journey home on foot before dark, she had to start now. Jael waited until it looked like the wild stallion had turned and moved away from her, then she headed for the main trade road that led from her home village to Ziaam.

A scream from the wild stallion let her know she had moved too soon. Jael fought the temptation to look back. Running was futile. Stopping now was suicide.

She had helped her father tame horses when she was a child and learned that slow, repetitive movements and sounds were a good trick for calming frightened or angry animals. She kept walking, sending up silent prayers to God to protect her, and concentrated on her breathing and steps to keep them steady and slow.

From the corner of her eye, she saw the image of a great black stallion charging toward her with eyes like flames of fire. She braced herself to leap out of the way and kept moving, fighting not to show in her movements that she was afraid. The beast was now upon her!

At the very last second, Jael leaped aside, out of the pathway of the charging horse. It barely missed her. She tumbled head over heels, getting dirt kicked up by the stallion's hooves in her face.

A memory flashed through her mind of a young black colt she had loved and befriended. Nightwind had refused to be tamed. Jael was the only one who could touch him or even get him to stand still for currying.

Her father had threatened a dozen times to sell him to the caravans passing by their village, but he had always given in to Jael's pleas to keep Nightwind. This horse was how she had pictured her beloved colt would be when he was fully mature.

Jael scrambled to get to her feet. She had no time to waste in memories or to miss the horse stolen when Zabed's men attacked her village. The stallion had turned and was already nearly upon her.

"Nightwind, I wish you were here," she cried.

The stallion jolted, breaking stride, and his head shot up. Snorting, he shook his head and picked up speed.

"Nightwind?" Jael cried, afraid to believe in the miracle granted to her.

Again, the stallion broke stride, this time shaking his entire body as he skipped sideways and came to a dead stop. He snorted with fury in his eyes and resumed charge.

"Nightwind! Nightwind! Chum-chum-yummy-yum," Jael chanted as loudly as she could, fighting to be heard over his hooves and the pounding of her heart.

She said the name again, only this time with the love she had for the horse as a young girl. She had always used the chanting of chum-chum-yummy-yum when she was not pleased with Nightwind's behavior.

"Nightwind, chum-chum-yummy-yum," she cried as the stallion reared high, forelegs kicking out. In just a heartbeat, those hooves would drive down on her and crush her to a pulp.

Nightwind twisted aside and came down hard on his forelegs, so the ground seemed to shudder underneath Jael's feet. He snorted and shook his head.

He stood so close to her that the ends of his tangled mane lashed her arm and face, stinging her. The fire left his eyes, replaced with confusion and surprise. He inhaled deeply, loudly, and tentatively touched her shoulder with his nose, then his tongue.

Jael kept chanting, "Nightwind! Chum-chum-yummy-yum!" She held still, wanting to fling her arms around the wild stallion, knowing this tentative recognition could be shattered and lost by any sudden movements.

Jael sent up silent prayers of thanks to God as she waited for Nightwind to remember her scent, sound, and taste. She watched the shuddering of all his muscles, listened to the snorting as he sniffed and sniffed again, and waited for the threat of imminent danger in his eyes to fade away.

Then the great black stallion stretched his neck slightly to nuzzle Jael as if to apologize, rubbing his nose and lips against her neck in a wet, ticklish kiss as he had done when he was a foal.

Quickly, Jael, with the nerve of a lioness, reached up as high as she could, hugged his neck, and kissed Nightwind with joy, calling his name over and over again.

Jael knew she had to take advantage of the moment. Testing the strength of Nightwind's memories, she rested one hand on his neck, stepped back, and with a commanding, calm voice, said, "Kneel, Nightwind. Kneel to Jael!"

Like a great warrior bowing down to his king, Nightwind went down upon his front legs before Jael. She did not waste any time.

As quick as a striking assassin, she leaped upon Nightwind's back, as she had done often as a young, restless maiden. Even though no one had ever ridden Nightwind but Jael, and some who had tried were dead, Nightwind had not forgotten his training.

He let out a loud cry, reared back, and took off running with Jael holding on for dear life. It had been years since she had ridden a horse without a saddle. Nightwind ran over the hills and through the valleys as though they did not exist.

Jael had seen Zabed the Terrible take Nightwind and all her father's horses when his men had raided her home and killed her parents. At some point, Nightwind must have broken free and lived as a wild stallion ever since.

They roamed through the hills and, several times, through the trees. Jael glimpsed mares and foals and knew these were Nightwind's herd.

As much as she wanted to take her childhood friend home with her, she knew her stallion was a wild thing and would fight for his freedom or die from the sickness of captivity if his love for her was strong enough to hold him. She thought of the mares and foals and knew she was being silly and sentimental, but she could not bear to take Nightwind away from his family that needed him for defense and leadership.

Jael thought, I will not take Nightwind away from here, but I must hurry home now. It is getting late and Heber will be looking for me. She chose a compromise. She would ride Nightwind as close to home as he would take her, set him free, and then go the rest of the way on foot.

Following the trade roads was foolish because there were men who would see the great untamed stallion on his journey home and try to capture him. Some of them would die, or Nightwind might die in his battle to stay free, so Jael kept to the hills and forests and ravines. She let herself forget her concerns, even her life as Heber's wife, and let herself enjoy these short hours of freedom on Nightwind's back.

Too soon, they came to the rolling grasslands between the last of the foothills and the city of Ziaam. The tent community where Heber's household camped sat halfway across the plain between the foothills and the city. Jael felt the tension that grew in Nightwind's muscles with each flying step closer to the signs of men.

This was their parting moment. She clung to him, half-afraid he had forgotten the old signal to stop; there were no reins to pull to make him stop. She sighed with regret, patted his neck one last time, and dismounted.

As Jael leaped from Nightwind's back to the ground, Nightwind looked at Jael as if to say, *Jael, what are you doing?* Jael gave Nightwind a hug and a goodbye kiss and started running for her home. The wind helped dry the tears that came despite her resolve to be strong and have no regrets.

Jael had barely covered half the distance to the tents when she heard a horse coming fast toward her. It was Nightwind!

As he came close, she could see his great eyes full of tender love, looking at her as if to say, *Now that I have found you, Jael, I will never again let you out of my sight!*

Jael's heart filled with love and compassion. She knew they would never be separated again. She hugged him, but instead of commanding him to kneel again, she grabbed handfuls of his mane and vaulted onto his back again.

"Go, Nightwind!" She cried. "Run, Nightwind, run!"

Their long run had wearied both of them, so Nightwind barely broke from a trot before they reached the tents. Several servants came running out at the sight of their mistress on a strange stallion, especially since she had left on a brown stallion late that morning. None of the men questioned her when Jael instructed them not to touch, try to bridle, or hobble Nightwind.

She led her old friend to a quiet area, within sight and smell of her tent, yet sheltered from the main noise and activities of the tents, and left him free to come and go as he chose. If Nightwind was not there in the morning, Jael told herself to be grateful for the joy they had shared today.

Now that her servants had seen her arrive on the stallion, word would spread that the huge black beast had an owner, and no one would try to steal it. Jael quietly laughed as she headed for her tent, knowing that anyone who tried to steal Nightwind would painfully regret it.

When Jael entered their tent, she was surprised to find Heber had not returned home. Then she saw the message she had left for him, sitting where she had left it, on his cushion by the brazier.

But where was Heber? Why wasn't he here?

Deep within her heart, she knew Heber was in serious trouble, for she remembered Bezer the Bully had warned her about a plot to kill Heber so that he would never be crowned king in Ziaam.

Jael made up her mind to go find him, yet Jael was smart. She knew she must disguise herself, for all of Ziaam knew her, and for a woman to tread on the streets of Ziaam at night was very dangerous, even after the concessions she had won after she triumphed in the New Moon Games.

Since night had fallen, Jael dressed all in black, even covering her face so that only her eyes were visible. She took several choice weapons and crept from her tent so no one would see her leave. Nightwind knew her despite her disguise and held still as she mounted. Then she commanded him to go.

It would be written upon the page of history books and in songs that it was not Heber's wife who rode toward Ziaam that night upon a great black stallion, but it was Jael the Conqueror, fully prepared to kill if anyone had done her Heber any harm.

Jael and Nightwind had not gone very far when they saw a horse without a rider coming slowly towards them. It was the horse that Heber always rode.

Fear gripped Jael's heart as she quickly leaped off Nightwind. The horse was covered by dried mud and briars and other signs of a long passage through rough territory.

She could only guess from the condition of the horse that it had traveled a long distance away from Ziaam, and that made no sense. Heber was to have gone into the city, not traveling the countryside around Ziaam.

She was relieved to see no blood or signs of damage on the saddle. Heber had not been attacked by bandits since then. But what had happened to him that he had separated from his horse?

The enemies Bezer had told her about had struck. But what had they done to Heber? Where was he?

Jael leaped onto Nightwind's back. Her fury and fear emerged as a scream of challenge, a yell that was not human but of an attacking beast.

Jael, the beautiful; Heber's precious diamond was no longer visible. In her place was another woman, an avenger. From behind her mask, her eyes burned like flames of fire. She kicked Nightwind in his sides with her feet and, with a strange, commanding voice, shouted, "Go! Go! Nightwind, go!"

Nightwind leaped forward with such speed and strength that it surprised even Jael. He ran faster than the wind, faster than he had

ever run before, as he carried his mistress towards her destiny as Jael
the Conqueror.

ZALBAZZAR THE SORCERER

Zalbazzar was the black sorcerer of Ziaam that ruled all the practitioners of magic in the surrounding countryside. He was the master of the black arts who had used his enchantments and powers to rule over Ziaam and the former king.

Some whispered that he was responsible for the former king's death, but they didn't whisper it too loudly for fear of Zalbazzar's vengeance. He lived beneath the palace in a room reached through a secret entrance and exit.

He knew his power came from Satan, his god. Zalbazzar was very old, yet he had a body of a 30-year-old man. He feared no man, beast, or giant upon the Earth, for what he could not kill with knives and poison, he could destroy with the power of witchcraft.

His constant companion and guard was Oog, his slave, half-man, and half-beast. Even without his sorcery, Zalbazzar feared no one because of Oog's brutal strength and skill in killing.

Just a few days ago, as they went through the forest, a great lion had attacked them. Oog, with the strength of five men, ripped out the lion's jaws with his bare hands and ate the lion's heart and inner organs.

Oog could understand the language of humans, but he could not speak any language, for he had the mouth and tongue of a reptile. His clawed feet were also weapons, and his deformed arms were stronger than any human and could turn in any position possible.

Oog lived in a cave next to the river that flowed not far from the palace, a short distance from Zalbazzar's secret chambers. He had been the sorcerer's slave since he was a small orphan boy, held prisoner by a curse cast upon him by Zalbazzar and Adah, Sisera's mother.

Zalbazzar had lived in Hazor until Jabin fell, and the power of the God of Israel had infiltrated the city, making it uncomfortable for him. Anyone who had supported King Jabin was hunted down by the Israelites.

He had come to Ziaam, disheartened by the deaths of Sisera and Adah, to lick his wounds and build up his strength and influence to punish Jael for killing them. He had decided Jael must die a horrible death, but even death wasn't punishment enough.

Even though Zalbazzar was a powerful sorcerer, he knew Jael was a worthy opponent. He would get revenge.

When Heber was proposed as a claimant to the throne of Ziaam, and he pitched his tents by the city's walls, Zalbazzar knew his time for revenge had come. First, he would punish Jael and cause her much pain and suffering by not allowing her husband to become king.

It infuriated him when he learned of Ikkesh's plan to kill Jael himself. That could not be allowed, because Zalbazzar wanted her punishment to come from his hands and no one else's. He hired Bezer to kill

Ikkesh and to capture or kill Heber. But he was not to harm Jael. Zalbazzar had special plans for that vixen.

Then, once Jael was disposed of, Zalbazzar decided it was time to deal with Barak and prophetess Deborah. Yet, when he thought of Deborah, a chill ran through his aged mind and wicked soul.

Yesterday, he had cast his spells and performed his enchantments. He knew his plan was working when he gazed into his scrying bowl.

Zalbazzar's thoughts were rudely interrupted by a knock on his secret door. With Oog at his side, he opened the door to find Bezer had arrived with the bodies of Ikkesh and Heber.

Zalbazzar could see that Ikkesh was dead, but Heber was still alive. He would have preferred Jael's husband to be dead as well, but torturing the man and making sure that Jael knew he had suffered before he died would give Zalbazzar added pleasure. The thought of that made him generous, so he paid Bezer twenty shekels of silver more than he had promised him.

"When shall I be crowned king?" Bezer asked.

"As soon as the council of elders hears that Heber and Jael are dead, which shall be very soon," he assured him.

As Bezer rode away from the palace, he wondered who would have the nerve to try to kill Jael. Well, he had done his job, and even though he loved money and the prospect of becoming king, he would never consider fighting Jael in hand-to-hand combat. Whether he won or lost, he would be humiliated for fighting a woman.

What interested him was the thought of convincing Jael to marry him once she had ended her mourning for Heber. Bezer remembered how it felt when Jael hugged him that morning, and he wanted more of it.

The thought of making her his wife and plaything, repaying her for beating him in that childhood fight, pleased him almost as much as the thought of being king.

Bezer decided he would begin his celebration now, instead of waiting for the council of elders to learn Heber was dead and offer him the crown under Zalbazzar's influence. He went straight to the most popular tavern in the city. He would buy every man there a drink and pay all the women there to dance before him, just as they would for a king.

"Yes, I am a king!" Bezer shouted. "King Bezer, I am King Bezer the Great! I shall be the king of Ziaam and the whole Kenite nation!"

THE BARAK ATTACK

As Jael entered Ziaam, she aimed for the most popular tavern, where she was sure to hear about Heber. As she crossed the open space around the well that served the shops and taverns in that part of the city, her attention was caught by two men fighting over a harlot.

Normally, Jael would try to speak to the woman to offer her help to leave her dangerous occupation. Tonight, she was too intent on finding Heber and rescuing him from the rumored enemies who wanted to keep him from becoming king.

She had nearly passed the three—the argument had escalated to the point where the men had grabbed each other's clothes and took turns shoving each other back and forth. The harlot looked bored. She glanced at Jael—her eyes widened a little at the sight of the figure dressed completely in black, even covering her face, then shrugged and turned back to the men.

"Neither of you will be worth anything if you keep this up. I'm going back into the tavern. I'll get twice as much coin from King Bezer as I will from you two." She sneered at the two men, who didn't react to her words but kept grunting, snarling, and shaking each other.

"King Bezer?" Jael said, reaching out to stop the harlot with a hand on her arm. "Heber is to be king, not Bezer."

"According to Bezer, he's going to be king as soon as the elders realize Heber isn't anywhere to be found." The woman's smile faded as she stared into Jael's black-masked face.

"He's been hinting that he knows where Heber is and that he's the one who made him vanish. He also claims he's the one who will tame Jael the Conqueror and put her back in her proper place as a woman." The harlot sniffed and shrugged.

"Men have no idea where a woman's proper place is, do they?"

"I know Bezer's proper place," Jael growled. The harlot paled and staggered back a step, shuddering at the fury in her voice and eyes.

"He is in the tavern?" Jael asked, barely waiting for the woman to nod before she strode around the well, aiming for the tavern.

The battling men staggered into her path. Jael drew her sword and gave them both a hard rap across the top of their heads with the pommel of her sword, making them stagger.

So it was Bezer who had captured and maybe killed Heber, my dear husband? Jael asked under her breath. *Well, I hope he is celebrating the joy of his heart, for tonight, he shall surely die.*

Like smoke, Jael disappeared into the darkness of the night and did not enter the tavern from the front door.

Meanwhile, Barak and Deborah were alarmed. They had received word from friends among the elders of the Kenites that Jael's husband did not show up for the meeting where he was to be pronounced king in Ziaam.

Barak still loved Jael deep within his heart, but due to the fact that she was Heber's wife, he could never express to anyone how he really felt about her. He would always be her secret admirer.

Barak went into Ziaam to learn what he could from several spies who kept him informed of all that went on in the ungodly side of that city. One man told him of rumors that the sorcerer Zalbazzar wanted to kill Heber so he could keep control over the city.

This spy had just come from a tavern where a ruffian named Bezer was celebrating, proclaiming himself king. The drunker he grew, the more blatant his hints that he had made Heber disappear.

As Barak entered the tavern, he saw Bezer and several other ruffians giving sport to the local harlots. One look at Bezer and Barak knew that despite the ruffian's drunken state, this would be a fight for his life.

Even if it cost him his life, Barak swore this ruffian would not become king in Heber's place. As he approached Bezer, challenging him to battle, calling him a coward and thief, three men who were friends of Bezer stood up with him, also with drawn swords.

Barak knew he was in serious trouble, more than he could handle. Out of nowhere, someone dressed in black, with a drawn sword and dagger, stood beside Barak. He took a quick glance, but didn't recognize Jael.

He had no more time to think as Bezer and his three friends attacked Jael and Barak with the force of trained warriors. Jael and Barak stood back-to-back. Barak's two opponents included Bezer.

Both men displayed great skill, despite being drunk. Barak could only imagine how deadly they were when sober. This battle would go down in history as one of the greatest tavern fights ever fought. Poems would be written about the "Barak Attack" and the mysterious woman dressed in black who fought like a lioness and swept through the room, defending herself as the best warrior anyone had ever seen.

Barak was very good, but Bezer was just as good. Jael could see Bezer setting a trap for Barak, using the other ruffian as a decoy. Bezer pretended to be wounded, causing Barak to pause for a moment.

Bezer stabbed Barak in the side, low in his ribs. Clapping a hand over the gush of blood and torn flesh, Barak was able to retaliate and drive his great sword through Bezer's heart. Both men fell down on the floor. The other three men immediately threw down their weapons and ran for their lives.

To the surprise of everyone there, Jael lifted Barak in her arms. Carrying him outside, she called for Nightwind. The people standing by jumped back in awe as the great black stallion came charging up to Jael from out of the shadows.

She commanded Nightwind to kneel, and setting Barak upon the horse, Jael leaped upon his back and commanded him to go. They ran into the night to the home of the prophetess Deborah. Jael knew if she did not get immediate help for Barak, he would surely die.

It might have been the blowing of the wind on Barak's face or the rough riding upon Nightwind that brought him back to consciousness. He knew that he was badly wounded, yet he could feel the arms of a woman holding him tight as Nightwind flew through the night.

Barak felt the strength of her arms around him and the shape of a woman pressed against his back and thought that if that was what dying was like, it wasn't so bad after all. He managed to open his eyes for just a moment, and looking over his shoulder, to his surprise, he saw the woman who held him was the same black-garbed and masked stranger who had fought so skillfully beside him.

"Do you know why Bezer attacked Heber? Do you know where he might have taken him?" The woman asked, her voice harsh with strain.

"Zalbazzar," Barak managed to say. He felt hot blood gushing fresh from his wound, and his head spun. The rocking motion of the galloping horse didn't help.

"Sorcerer wants to control..." he fought for breath and struggled against the blackness creeping across his vision. He wanted to talk to her and thank her, but no more words would come. Then there was darkness. Losing consciousness, he knew nothing at all.

When Jael arrived at the home of Deborah, the judge of Israel, she knew that this was not the time for anyone to know who she was. Barak was unconscious, and she was grateful for the reprieve as she slid him from Nightwind's back and laid the wounded Barak down in front of the door.

She knocked loudly upon Deborah's door. When she heard footsteps coming, Jael leaped onto Nightwind's back and fled into the night.

When Deborah opened the door, Jael was already gone. Deborah could hear the sound of a running horse going fast toward Ziaam. The Spirit of God touched her heart, and she knew the rider was Jael. Answers to the questions of how Barak had been wounded and why Jael had brought him here and fled would have to be answered later.

Deborah tugged aside Barak's bloody, torn clothes to see his wounds while calling for her servants. She thanked Jehovah that several of her servants had skill in healing.

As two strong men picked up Barak to bring him into the house, Deborah raised her hands to the night sky and prayed to Jehovah to spare Barak's life and to keep her friend Jael safe. She knew that her

God knew all things, and there was nothing impossible for Him to do.

Returning to Ziaam, Jael did not go back into the city. She had heard about the sorcerer Zalbazzar and the rumors that he lived in the palace, making it easier to control the former king. She shuddered at the thought of such a man living in her future home if Heber succeeded in being named king.

She vowed that, on that night, the palace would be cleaned of all its foul inhabitants. Even though Jael didn't know what lay in front of her when she reached the palace or even how she would find Zalbazzar's lair, she knew one thing: whoever harmed her husband would pay with his life.

As Heber regained consciousness and opened his eyes, an exploding pain in his head took his breath away. It felt like he laid for hours breathing shallowly, trying not to cry out.

Tentative movements of his fingers, then gingerly stretching out his hands and arms, showed him before he even opened his eyes that he lay in a cramped cage. From the smell of dampness and stone, the sound of torches crackling, and some strange, noxious odor that thickened the air, he guessed his prison was underground.

But where? Who had attacked him?

He could guess why: one of the other claimants for kingship among the Kenites had decided he was the winner and attacked him to take him out of the contest.

Finally, the pain in the back of Heber's head faded enough that he dared to open his eyes. He lay facing into the room. Only a few steps away from him, Heber saw a man dressed in royal robes, spattered with blood and embroidered with symbols of all the gods of the Canaanites.

It was easy to guess this man was some kind of priest or magic worker. He was a man in his prime, handsome and strong, but a stranger. He stood in front of a brazier sitting on a table, stirring a bowl of something that smoked and gave off a pungent, noxious odor.

Heber had heard the rumors of a mysterious sorcerer named Zalbazzar, who had power over the previous king. He could only guess he now saw the man and was his prisoner.

Heber turned his head to learn more about his prison. What he saw next made him groan out loud in awe and disgust.

Over in the corner of the room was Oog, who had cut open the dead body of Ikkesh and was feasting on his inward parts. It made Heber's skin crawl when he saw Oog's reptilian head and webbed feet with great claws that tore the body of Ikkesh apart and the gore that dripped from the monster's mouth as he devoured the dead man.

When they heard Heber moan, Oog and Zalbazzar ran over to his cage.

'Well, well, well!" Taunted Zalbazzar.

"How is the king of Ziaam doing today? You are surely in your palace but not on your throne," he laughed at the irony of his words.

Oog slapped his webbed hands together, his eyes sparkling with malice and his fanged jaws parting in silent laughter. His long tongue slithered out like a lizard tasting its prey in the air, and Heber imagined the monster anticipated eating him when it was finished with Ikkesh.

Suddenly, the torches guttered and dimmed, plunging the room into shadows, and the stink of Zalbazzar's potion was smothered by a stench that took everyone's breath away. Zalbazzar let out a scream as the door swung open, and a huge snake with the head of a man entered the room.

The sorcerer paled and staggered backward, reaching out to brace himself against the table. The room turned colder than ice.

"Who...who...who...are you?" Zalbazzar stuttered as he cried out in fear.

As Satan pulled his huge frame into the room, Oog, acting in fear, made a fatal mistake. He reached out his hands to defend himself.

Satan opened his mouth wide and faster than the eye could see, devouring Oog in one gulp. Turning to face the trembling Zalbazzar and Heber, who were praying to God for help, Satan transformed himself into a handsome man-like being.

"I am Satan, your god, the god of this world, the prince of demons, and the power of the air."

Heber fainted, overcome by the cold and stench. His last conscious thought was a prayer to God to protect Jael against their enemies.

"You have served me these many years," Satan continued. "Bow down and worship me; kiss my hands and my feet!"

Zalbazzar was nauseous from the stench, and he saw Satan's hands and feet were filthy with refuse. The stench grew stronger with every second.

Remembering Oog, Zalbazzar fought the urge to vomit, and falling down, began to kiss Satan's hands and his feet that had not been washed in thousands of years. Satan was well pleased.

Jael had approached the palace surrounded by prayers: her own and the ones sent up by Deborah. A single beam of moonlight penetrated the clouds and shone down on the riverbank behind the palace, showing a faint path through the trees.

Sending up a prayer of thanks, she guided Nightwind down that path until it grew too thin for the massive stallion to pass, then she went on foot until she found the gap in the bedrock that supported the palace.

The gap opened into a passageway under the palace. Jael came to an open doorway with stairs leading into the palace.

The stench rolling out of that open doorway was incredible and made her stagger. Bracing herself, she entered the room with her drawn sword and dagger. What she saw made her mind reel, and her heart stop beating.

She saw Satan standing and Zalbazzar worshipping at his feet, and her dear Heber locked in a cage, looking like he was dead. Jael knew from her studies Satan's assignment, power and purpose, and her authority over him. She immediately rebuked him in the name of Jehovah, her God, and commanded him to flee and be gone.

While Satan did not fear Jael or any human being, he greatly feared the God she served. Immediately, he exploded into a white cloud of dust and disappeared.

Zalbazzar, not understanding the power of a believer, was amazed. He thought it was black magic that Jael used over Satan, his god. He believed he could gain much more power with Satan if he killed Jael.

Cursing and chanting spells, he drew his knife and sword and ran toward Jael to cut off her head, but to his amazement, Jael was not there!

"Nobody is that fast," he snarled in disbelief. He ran out into the passageway to chase her.

As he located her on the stairway leading upstairs, Zalbazzar drew poison darts from the case on his belt and flung two at Jael faster than he had ever thrown them before. No man had ever survived his poisonous darts! It was his last mistake.

Jael caught the first one, and avoiding the second, she threw the poisonous dart, which hit its mark on Zalbazzar's neck. He was dead before he hit the floor.

Quickly, Jael ran to Heber and, with one great swing of her sword, cut the bars of the cage asunder. Seeing that Heber was alive and slowly regaining consciousness caused tears to fill Jael's eyes.

Oh, how she loved that man. She wanted to hold him, console him, kiss him, and see him safely home. She knew that was not possible, for she did not yet want Heber to know her secret life as Jael the Conqueror.

Jael lifted him up and helped him to walk outside, and guided him up the riverbank to where he could see the city before him and the palace behind him.

"Can you find your way home from here?" She asked, lowering her voice and making it rough so he would not recognize her. She was thankful she still wore her mask.

"Yes, I can, thank you. Who...?" Heber turned, trying to see Jael's face, but she slipped into the night and vanished. He heard the sound of a running horse, but when he looked, all he could see was a large black horse and its rider fading into the night along the riverbank.

Feeling weak, tired, and completely worn, Heber headed home to where he knew Jael would be waiting for him with open arms. Concern for her and fear that his enemies had attacked her as well gave him strength, steadiness, and speed.

Jael hurried home, grateful for Nightwind's speed. She left him in the sheltered grassy area they had left just a few short hours ago and hurried into her tent. She washed and changed her clothes quickly and was standing in the doorway when Heber came stumbling towards her.

Jael ran to him and helped him inside and onto their bed. She washed his wounded head, hugging and kissing him, with tears flowing down her face.

Heber told her of his capture and imprisonment, of a great woman dressed in black who had rescued him from death. Jael vowed that someday she would tell Heber about her adventure that night and her call by God as a warrior.

Jael's kisses upon Heber's face were the best medicine, and her gentle hands seemed to drive away all of his pains. They spent the night in the solace of lovemaking and intimate romance, greater than ever before.

Less than a month later, the elders of the Kenites announced that Heber had been chosen as the next king. There was joy in Ziaam, and people from miles around came to congratulate Heber and Jael, to offer them their full support.

Everywhere they went, people would gather around them and follow after them, promising to be good citizens of their kingship.

CHAPTER 15
ALL HAIL TO THE KING AND QUEEN

It was a great day in the city of Ziaam, the capital city of the Kenite nation, where thousands of people from all nations and tongues were gathered together for the coronation of Heber as king and Jael as queen. There was merrymaking, dancing, singing, and every type of entertainment possible.

As Jael sat beside Heber upon the throne and the coronation began, she couldn't help but weep as she thought about her deceased parents and her Aunt Modessa, wishing they could have been beside her, and yet she knew that if things had not happened the way that they did, she would not have been there herself.

Her thoughts were interrupted by thousands who repeatedly chanted and shouted, "Hail to Heber the King" and "Hail to Jael the Queen," with all their might.

It was a three-day celebration that would go down in Kenite history as one of the greatest coronations ever. The kings of many countries were there.

It was a fascinating and intoxicating event, with so many wondrous gifts that filled the largest room in the palace. Deborah, the judge, was Jael's precious guest, and Lapidoth, her husband, was Heber's honor guard for three days of celebration.

Finally, it was all over. Heber and Jael were all alone in the royal bedchamber.

Instead of taking Jael into his arms, he came closer to her, looked deeply into her eyes, and said, "Jael, my queen, there is no woman in all the earth like you. You are the most beautiful woman that I have ever seen. I am so proud to be your husband, and I promise to be the best king in this world for you. You are my heart, my joy, the apple of my eye. I have no need of spoil."

Jael replied, saying, "Heber, there is no man like you. You satisfy my every need and fulfill my heart's desire. Just one touch of your tender hands and one kiss upon my lips, and I am in another world. You are my champion, my mighty warrior, who my soul loves."

Heber said, "Your love is better than the best wine, and your fragrance is a bundle of myrrh, even as a cluster of flowers from the Mountains of Engedi."

Jael replied, "I want you to lie between my breasts, my beloved, all night long and fulfill your need for love. Oh, let us soar above the clouds together, even higher than the stars in the sky, until the morning light, when the shadows flee away, and love can speak no more."

Heber said, "You have doves' eyes, and your cheeks are lovely as rows of jewels, and your neck is sweeter than the finest honeycomb. You are my lily of the valley, and your hair is softer than the hair of a young roe or a young lamb."

When Jael tried to let Heber know that she was his, that the rivers of desire within her soul overflowed, Heber's emotions consumed his mind, and the fire within his soul ravished his heart. He entered his glory, and they shared the utopia of lovemaking until the breaking of another day.

ALL IS WELL THAT ENDS WELL

Barak was very pleased that Heber was the king of the Kenite nation and Jael was his queen. He was very happy for both of them.

Even though he truly loved Jael, he knew he could never have her. Barak was sure that if he could just find the woman dressed in black who fought at his side against Bezer, the Bully, and saved his life, he would surely ask for her hand in marriage, regardless of her race.

Why, she was just marvelous, wonderful! He remembered how valiantly she had fought that night and her strong yet tender arms that held him as they rode madly through the night to Deborah's house.

And what a horse she rode! A great black stallion carried them both across the land as if they weren't even there! Well, he would surely spend many days searching for her until he found her, he vowed.

Barak soon found her. There came a day when the leaders of Israel met with the king and queen of the Kenites nation to discuss the uniting and fellowship of both nations and the great temple that Heber the king had planned to build in Ziaam to worship the true and living God. The meeting was such a success; everyone was in high spirits and embraced at the end.

The moment Barak hugged Jael and her arms went around his waist, he knew these were the same arms that had held him as they rode through the night, that it was Jael who fought at his side, dressed in black, and who had saved his life! Quickly, before Jael or anyone else could see the love in his eyes or the tears that began to flow from them, Barak excused himself.

Mounting his horse, he went straight to the home of Deborah, the judge of Israel. When Deborah opened the door and saw Barak, she could tell he had something on his mind.

"Deborah," Barak said, "I have been the captain of your army for many years. I have never commanded anything from you, but now I want you to tell the truth. Tell me all that you know about Jael, the wife of Heber, the king of the Kenite nation."

Deborah made Barak swear to keep silent and to tell no one else for as long as he lived. He agreed.

Deborah told him all that she knew. The story that she told touched Barak's heart so much that both of them began to sing and write more songs about Jael the Conqueror, songs that would be sung throughout the land for hundreds of years. Songs of a mighty warrior, a heroine dressed in black, who went throughout the Kenite nation at night on a mighty horse, saving many from hurt, harm, and danger. A godly woman who helped the poor and needy and brought law and order to the land, even Canaan. No one knew except Barak and Deborah.

During the day, as queen, a multitude of people often followed Jael and loved her, saying that she was the best queen of all. For years, Heber didn't know that the horse that pulled Queen Jael's chariot was Nightwind, the great horse that he had seen that day when Jael had rescued him from Satan and Zalbazzar, the sorcerer.

Heber was honored and respected as king of the Kenite nation. All the other kings respected him and were at peace with him.

He built a great army of over 100,000 men, and because the Kenite people were workers of metal, the king's soldiers had the best weapons. Besides all this, there were stories told and songs sung about a woman dressed in black, a goddess who watched over the Kenite people and could slay a thousand men in battle.

Jael the Conqueror, the queen of the Kenite nation, bore three sons and two daughters, who grew up to be men and women of great honor and character to serve Jehovah the Lord God. Zana, the eldest daughter, and Hebron, the youngest son, became even greater warriors and conquerors than their parents.

Heber lived to be 120 years old, and Jael 117 years old. One day, their sons found them both in their bedchamber, deceased, with their arms holding each other tight. The tombstone that people saw for 300 years as they passed by the place where Jael lay read: "Here lies Jael the Conqueror, God's jewel and Heber's diamond, blessed above women."

THE END

NOTES

5. JAEL, BLESSED ABOVE WOMEN

1. Goode, ~ Richard. (2019, June 6). *Wild goat/ibex – day 6 of 30 days [biblically] wild*. Newman Research Centre for the Bible and its Reception. https://bibleresearchto-day.com/2019/06/06/wild-goat-ibex-day-6-of-30-days-biblically-wild.

6. DEBORAH THE PROPHETESS

1. Keegan Publications, A Division of Kregal Inc. (1990). Names by Alfred S. Jones. In Jones' Dictionary of Old Testament.
2. *H8559 - tāmār - strong's hebrew lexicon (KJV)*. Blue Letter Bible. (n.d.). https://www.blueletterbible.org/lexicon/h8559/kjv/wlc/0-1.
3. Abarim Publications. (n.d.). *The amazing name Jabin: Meaning and etymology*. Abarim Publications. https://www.abarim-publications.com/Meaning/Jabin.html#:~:text=Jabin%20meaning,reads%20He%20(God)%20Perceives.
4. Oxford University Press: *Sisera*. Helps to the study of the bible - christian classics ethereal library. (n.d.). https://ccel.org/ccel/oxford/ helps/helps.xlvi.html.

FUTURE PLANS FOR SISERA, THE GIANT

1. Keegan Publications, A Division of Kregal Inc. (1990). Names by Alfred S. Jones. In Jones' Dictionary of Old Testament.

ABOUT THE AUTHOR

Bishop Dr. Donald Downing is the author of 37 books. He considers *Jael the Conqueror* to be his best authorship, equal to the classic book, *Hidden Treasures of the Heart*.

His passionate desire is to see pure, clean hearts in every family, church, and nation unto God. Learn more about him, his writings, and his ministry at:

http://heartdoctordowning.com.

www.ingramcontent.com/pod-product-compliance
Lightning Source LLC
Chambersburg PA
CBHW051516120626
46551CB00012B/942